The Wealth Dragon Way

The Wealth Dragon Way

THE WHY, THE WHEN AND THE HOW TO BECOME INFINITELY WEALTHY

John Lee
Vincent Wong

WILEY

Cover design: Wiley

Published by John Wiley & Sons Singapore Pte. Ltd.

1 Fusionopolis Walk, #07-01, Solaris South Tower, Singapore 138628

Other Wiley Editorial Offices
John Wiley & Sons, 111 River Street, Hoboken, NJ 07030, USA
John Wiley & Sons, The Atrium, Southern Gate, Chichester, West Sussex, P019 8SQ, United Kingdom
John Wiley & Sons (Canada) Ltd., 5353 Dundas Street West, Suite 400, Toronto, Ontario, M9B 6HB, Canada
John Wiley & Sons Australia Ltd., 42 McDougall Street, Milton, Queensland 4064, Australia
Wiley-VCH, Boschstrasse 12, D-69469 Weinheim, Germany

ISBN 978-1-119-07783-1 (Paperback)
ISBN 978-1-119-07785-5 (ePDF)
ISBN 978-1-119-07784-8 (ePub)
ISBN 978-1-119-07786-2 (oBook)

Set in 11/13pt Baskerville by Aptara Inc., New Delhi, India

Printed in Singapore by C.O.S. Printers Pte. Ltd.

10 9 8 7 6 5 4 3 2 1

For Annika and Jennifer

Contents

Preface

We're going to discuss *why* to become wealthy extensively in this book, so we'd like to start by asking you this question: *Why* did you pick up this book? We're guessing it's because you'd like to have more money in your life. We can definitely show you *how* to achieve this, but *why* do you want more money in your life? We're assuming it's so you don't have to worry about whether you'll always be able to afford to pay the bills. *Why* do you want to be free of money worries? Presumably so that you're able to spend more time and energy on the things and people you value. So, *when* do you want to start living like this? That's a question only you can answer.

We started Wealth Dragons in 2009, hoping we could educate people about wealth creation and help them realize their full potential. Our specific expertise lies in different areas of the property business, but over the years we have explored other avenues of passive income generation and asset building as we have continued along the path of our own education. We pass on anything and everything new that we learn, that we believe will enrich the lives of others, in our seminars and educational programmes. We, like you, are constantly learning and growing. Since we started the company we have given countless seminars and have taught wealth creation programmes that are constantly evolving, all over the world.

One of our key ambitions has always been to reach as wide an audience as possible, and this is what inspired us to write a book. Our aim in this book is to give you, the reader, an overview of our philosophies about wealth creation, share with you our own personal stories, and inspire you to further your own wealth education.

Over the years we've received a great deal of positive feedback from our clients students and business associates. We hope this book will also remind them of why they chose us and why they stuck with us.

While we have written the book together, with a joint voice for the most part, we obviously have our individual stories and thoughts to share. This will be clearly indicated in the text.

If this is your first introduction to Wealth Dragons, we hope it inspires you and gives you plenty to think about. Of course, it goes without saying that we would love to hear from you, and we invite you to come and meet us at a seminar sometime in the future. You'll find all the relevant contact details at the back of the book.

We can't wait to meet you when you're ready to become a wealth dragon!

Acknowledgments

We are indebted to so many people who have helped make and shape this book. First, we are very grateful to the John Wiley & Sons team, including Kimberly Monroe-Hill, Jeremy Chia, Gladys Ganaden, and especially Nick Wallwork and Nazneen Halim, who championed the book from the start. To our families and friends, we extend our deepest gratitude for all their ongoing love and support. We wouldn't be where we are today without the hard work and support of our entire Wealth Dragons team, including our administration and sales teams, and our speakers, who all help make our business so successful and the daily grind so enjoyable. They are all a part of this journey, as they are the ones who really start the process of changing people's lives. We would also like to thank Miranda Leslau for all her expertise. But the people to whom we owe the greatest debt are those who have inspired so much of the material in this book . . . our students. They help us learn while we teach. This book is a testament to them. Many of them started out believing they didn't have choices in life. To anyone who has been told they can't achieve something, we have written this book to tell you that you can.

About the Authors

John Lee is the CEO and co-founder of Wealth Dragons. John started investing in property in his early twenties. By the time he was 27, John had achieved his goal of becoming a self-made millionaire. His experiences inspired him to share his knowledge with others and he was soon teaching seminars in property investment throughout the United Kingdom. He subsequently gained an international reputation as a motivational speaker and has shared stages with former US President Bill Clinton, Alan Sugar, Richard Branson, Jack Welch (ex-CEO of GE) and Randa Zuckerberg (co-founder of Facebook). John also trains people to become world-class public speakers. He has helped several of his students build highly successful businesses and achieve international acclaim. John's success came despite a humble start in life. He was born to Chinese parents who ran a takeaway restaurant in the north of England. All of John's achievements came as the result of endless hard work and unwavering tenacity. John is dedicated to showing others how they have the opportunity to do the same and is continually inspired by watching his students achieve the kind of success they thought they could only ever dream of.

* * *

Vincent Wong is the COO and co-founder of Wealth Dragons. Vince is one of the most dynamic and well-respected property entrepreneurs in the United Kingdom and internationally. As well as building his own multimillion-pound property portfolio, Vince has helped countless people source and structure property deals through his property companies. At the height of the financial crisis, Vince pioneered groundbreaking financing strategies and was successful in getting lease options legalized for residential property sales in the United Kingdom, Malaysia and the Netherlands (and is currently working with regulators on campaigns in Poland and Singapore).

Vince personally mentors a number of property investors and business owners. He is an internationally recognized public speaker and expert in the property industry and he is regularly invited to speak to audiences of more than 1,000 at the prestigious Property Outlook Conference in Kuala Lumpur, Malaysia (the biggest property conference in Asia). Vince is a graduate of the University of London's School of Pharmacy and holds an MBA from Cass Business School.

Introduction: The Story of Wealth Dragons

In three words I can sum up everything I've learned about life: It goes on.

—Robert Frost

John: My rather ordinary, humble start in life took place in a small Lancashire town in the north of England, not far from the Yorkshire Dales. I was born in Burnley General Hospital in 1981 and grew up in Colne, a fairly remote and typically northern English town, where my parents owned and ran the local Chinese takeaway. They were both originally from Hong Kong and moved to the UK in the 1970s. They married shortly after meeting and started what was to become a family business. Many Chinese people born in Hong Kong moved to the UK in those days, taking advantage of the time during which Hong Kong was a British territory, which gave them the right to British nationality. The influx was responsible for a surge in Chinese takeaways. The British seemed to love the new, exotic, tasty (and relatively cheap) fast food, and many families built up successful small businesses as a result.

My parents, and their extended family members, worked long hours to keep the business up and running, and making a profit. It was a hard life and I hardly saw them while I was growing up. Colne has grown since the time I lived there, but during my childhood there were only a handful of shops and one primary school, where I was teased mercilessly for being the only Chinese boy in the school. I remember my nickname was Bruce Lee. This might have been a compliment within a big group of Chinese kids who worshipped the martial arts hero, but the way in which the local English kids used it when they directed it at me was definitely derogatory. They would do karate moves in front of me and laugh. I once got flying-kicked in the back so hard that it knocked me off my feet. When I took off my jacket I found there was the imprint of a shoe on it. I don't remember having any real friends at school and I don't think I went to more than two or three birthday parties throughout my entire school years. Even when I became a teenager and the kids in my area started going out to parties and local clubs, I missed out because my parents wouldn't allow me to go. Anytime I wasn't at school I was expected to work in the takeaway.

I started working in the takeaway—doing odd jobs, cleaning and carrying things around—at around the age of seven or eight years old. I got a little pocket money for the mundane jobs I did. Everyone worked in the family business, and I knew it was expected that my brother and I would take it over some day.

But I had other plans.

I had watched my parents work night and day in a business that gave them a modest living and prevented them from spending quality time with their children. They worked seven days a week, so my brother and I were mostly raised by our aunts and uncles. I always knew I wanted a different life. Not only did I want to give my future children more options (including the option to spend time with their father), but I also wanted to help my parents get more time to enjoy life without working every waking minute. I wanted to free them from the chains that bound them to their arduous existence.

By the time I started college I was working three different jobs. I was making money in every way I could, in every spare minute I could find. Along with working in the takeaway most evenings, I got a weekend job in a shoe shop. I also signed up for part-time telesales work, which was brutal. It involved cold-calling people listed in the Yellow Pages to sell them web sites. I got rejection after rejection; it was soul-destroying. But in hindsight it was invaluable experience as it instilled a high tolerance for rejection in me, which served me well later in life! My inspiration was my determination to break free from the future that had been laid out for me—a future identical to the life my parents led. I respected them, but I didn't want to live like them. I wanted to reach for more; I believed I could achieve more.

Those were some tough years. I had absolutely no life and no friends; at times I resented it, but I knew I had to keep going. I became obsessed with working, believing I could work my way to success. But I was frustrated by how much time it took to make a modest amount of money. Was I even doing anything different from my parents, in giving up all my time to make money? That feeling probably planted the first seed of my determination to find a way to buy back my time, to make significant money without it taking up all of my time. That growing feeling—the deep desire for the freedom to do what I wanted with my time, whilst still earning an income—helped motivate me in the years to come.

I did well enough at school to get into university; I got a place at the University of Hull to study computer animation. With what my parents had put aside for my higher education, and with the money I'd saved from all my jobs, I was able to study full-time without having to work to supplement my allowance. Being away from home and out of the grind of working in the takeaway for the first time in my life, I also had my first taste of a real social life. It was great. I made some good friends and found a little self-confidence. But money was still tight and I couldn't wait to graduate and move down south where I believed I could command a better salary than my peers.

My first job was close to London, in Guildford. My starting salary was £21,000, while most of my friends were in jobs that paid them around £15,000; I definitely felt their jealousy. However, I soon discovered that their jealousy was largely unfounded, because the reality of earning £21,000 was not as rosy as I thought it would be. By the time I'd paid my rent and all my living costs in the expensive London commuter belt, I had less money than I did when I was doing menial work in Yorkshire!

I lasted about a year in that first job and then jumped around doing some freelance contracts for a while before landing my next big job at an animation company called Criterion. I started on a salary of £26,000 and was convinced that this increase was going to change my life. But with more money coming in I was soon spending more on going out and enjoying myself, and it wasn't long before I found I had even *less* money left at the end of the month than before!

My next job was my dream job.

My best friend at university had been Darren Rodriguez. We had both been obsessed with working as hard as we could. We used to get up at 5 A.M. to wait outside the main building until the caretaker let us in. We were the first to get in and always the last to leave. We regularly told anyone who would listen that it was our ambition to get jobs at Framestore, the computer animation company that was fast on its way to working on Oscar-winning films such as the Harry Potter films and *Avatar.* All our fellow students thought we were being overly ambitious. Jobs at Framestore were highly coveted and competition was fierce, so no one believed we would get in there. Their negativity made us even more determined. We never gave up, and only a few years after we graduated, Darren landed his job there. I secured my position soon after leaving Criterion.

But as is so often the case when you realize your dream, after an initial honeymoon period we became bored and frustrated. We started to hate our purported dream jobs just like we'd ended up dissatisfied with all our other jobs. We were frustrated with the hours, the politics, and (again) that feeling that we never had enough money, despite the fact that we were both earning considerably more than most of our friends.

I started at Framestore on a salary of a whopping £36,000. This time I was sure I was fast on my way to living the high life. But, just as before, I soon discovered my pay cheque got eaten up pretty quickly. My travelling costs went up as I was now commuting from Guildford, where I still lived, into central London, plus I spent a proportionally higher amount on other expenses. I got a new car with a short-term loan, a laptop, some nice clothes, and suddenly I was back to square one . . . struggling (relatively speaking) to make ends meet. I couldn't believe I was burning through all my money. I worked out my monthly budget and discovered that, after deducting bills, I had £27 in disposable income that I could spend each day. One lunch in a nice restaurant in the city, or a round of drinks for a few friends (who perceived me as being much wealthier than them), would wipe that out in an hour.

Darren was equally frustrated. We used to meet in the canteen every lunchtime and during all our coffee breaks to plot our escape from the rat race. We were strategizing together, in order to figure out how we could literally buy back our time. We were two guys in our midtwenties who were already heavily disillusioned with life. Something was wrong with that picture!

One day, close to my birthday, Darren presented me with an early birthday present. It was a book. I will never forget the look of excitement on his face. He told me that this was it; this was how we were going to break free. He knew I was dyslexic, that it was a real struggle for me to read anything, but he begged me to read the book cover to cover, and as soon as I could. The book was *Rich Dad, Poor Dad* by Robert Kiyosaki.

I opened the book on the tube on the way home and didn't put it down for two days. I was gripped. It was my first introduction to the concept of passive income, and I became obsessed with it. Darren and I could not stop talking about how we were going to achieve our new goals of creating a passive income source that would allow us to keep building our wealth indefinitely. I could hardly believe that so much financial security and freedom was available to me and I became 100 percent focused on working out how I could make it happen.

During the months that followed, all Darren and I did was research the topic. We attended countless seminars and trawled the Internet looking for new strategies for building passive income. Of course the one that consistently stood out was earning a rental income from a property portfolio, so we concentrated our efforts on learning everything we could about property investment.

Suddenly my three-hour-round-trip commute became valuable learning time for me. I added a costly (at the time) 3G plan to my mobile phone package so that I could use a dongle on my laptop—smartphones still being fairly cost-prohibitive for the average person in those days—and carry on researching online during my commute. I would even walk through the West End to work rather than taking the tube, carrying my laptop and reading as I walked so that I could stay online.

And then the day came when I had a big choice presented to me. It was a crossroads of sort and would determine the direction of the next period of my life.

I had been listening to every motivational tape I could get my hands on. I was listening to Anthony Robbins on repeat, and I'd just discovered Dolf de Roos—the New Zealand property millionaire and best-selling author. I had been listening to an audiobook by de Roos on the day I received a call from a rival animation company that was trying to poach me away from Framestore. They were prepared to offer me a starting salary of £60,000. That same day I heard Dolf de Roos describe a moment in his life when he came to a crossroads. He was offered a job paying $30,000 on the same day that he made a $30,000 profit on a property. He asked himself why he should invest a year's worth of his time to earn $30,000 when he'd just made $30,000 in one day. He turned the job offer down and became a full-time property investor. His experience and decision inspired me; I called the other animation company, turned down the £60,000 job offer, and my fate was sealed. I now knew what I had committed myself to focusing on.

I will never forget that day, that moment, when I was listening to the Dolf de Roos audiobook and made that life-changing decision. I'd been listening to it in a café during a lunch break and on the way back to the office I ran into Darren. I told him that I'd come to a major decision; that I'd decided I was going to quit my job. He didn't believe me, so to prove it, as soon as I was back at my desk, I wrote an e-mail and sent it to the whole office. I said it was my last day at Framestore and anyone who felt like going for drinks after work should join me at the local pub so we could say our good-byes. My boss was at my desk in minutes, asking if it was a joke. I told him I was serious.

Because of the confidential nature of the projects we were working on at the time, Framestore had to give me a month's garden leave (which means you remain on the company payroll through your official notice period but are barred from coming into the office or working for another employer; you effectively have to sit at home!). Sending that e-mail did feel a little mad, but I knew it would force me into action, that there would be no going back, that I would have to go through with my plan. It was amazing how much freedom I felt immediately; it was like a weight lifting off me. I knew I'd done the right thing and I never looked back.

I remember waking up the day after I quit with a feeling of total euphoria. Suddenly I had what I wanted: I had my time back. The whole day stretched out in front of me; I could spend all that time continuing my research. I also knew that if I played my cards right, the rest of my life could be like this: being able to choose how I spent my time each day. No one owned my time anymore. It felt fantastic. I dedicated every waking moment to going to seminars and doing research on passive income generation. Of course I kept the fact I'd quit my job quiet from my friends and family for a while!

I knew I had to get started in property investment as soon as possible. I had a short window in which I still had a salary that I could use to secure a mortgage. In 2005 it was definitely easier to get a mortgage than it is today, but I still needed to prove my earnings; I had to get a mortgage while I was still on garden leave from Framestore. I started researching mortgage brokers. And that's how I came across Ying Tan.

Ying lived near me in Guildford so I went to see him, to speak to him about getting into the property business. He offered to mentor me. When I asked him how much he charged, he said £10,000. I nearly fell off my chair. I asked him how he could justify that price. He told me that what I would learn in two days would set me up for life; that he would show me a revolutionary way of buying property that could completely change my life. I instinctively felt I had to do it. But how was I going to get that much money? The only thing I had that was worth that much was my car. I had a Honda S2000 that I knew I could get around £10,000 for. The question was, should I use that £10,000 as a deposit for one property or pay Ying Tan to mentor me? I was young; I guess I was ready to live dangerously!

The few friends I mentioned my plan to thought I was crazy. They were convinced it was some scam and that I was about to be ripped off. But I kept talking to Ying and he kept reassuring me. In the end he offered me a deal. He said I could pay him half of the money up front and the other half when my first property deal went through. I was still petrified and I nearly pulled out several times. It seemed like such a huge sum of money. However, at one point I divided it by 365 days and realized it was around £27 a day, the exact sum I used to have as disposable income when I worked at Framestore. That made it more manageable to think about; it made it relatively acceptable, as if all I was doing was making the decision to go without a year's worth of expensive lunches! Doing that calculation somehow helped me to make my final decision to move forward.

I had never been so scared in my life. Handing over all that money was still incredibly painful. But the pain of the thought of having my newfound freedom taken away was greater. I never wanted to go back to being an employee. I wanted to be in control of how I spent my time for the rest of my life. I'd tasted that freedom and wasn't prepared to give it up again.

Ying was as good as his word. Through a loophole in property financing at the time, he'd figured out that if you bought a property at a significant discount and then immediately refinanced it, you could make an immediate cash sum. The banks subsequently closed this particular loophole, specifying that you have to own a property for six months before refinancing, but for a while there was a decent profit to be made by doing the type of deals Ying had taken advantage of.

My first property deal made me £9,000. Ying helped me find a property that was valued at £250,000. I managed to negotiate a discount with the owner/developer and agreed to buy it for £200,000, which I financed through a bridging loan. As soon as the property was mine, I refinanced it, taking out a mortgage of £212,500 (85 percent). This was a relatively quick and simple process. Before the global financial crisis hit, lenders were falling over themselves to offer mortgages to anyone, regardless of their means to pay it back. I paid off the £200,000 bridging loan and had £12,500 left over. After paying off my costs and a small amount of interest on the short-term bridging loan, I had around £9,000 left.

I appreciated everything Ying taught me. He was an expert at finding loopholes to make money from and I carried on using him to broker mortgages on my future properties. But I needed more; I wanted to explore every source of experience and information out there. I needed other skills if I was going to be as successful as I aimed to be. I needed expert marketing and negotiating skills. I wanted to soak up as much education as I could find. I discovered a property networking group that was offering a course costing £3,500. Even though my investment with Ying had paid off, I was apprehensive about risking a big chunk of money again, so I went to talk to my Uncle Chi.

Like my parents, and so many other Chinese people of his generation, my Uncle Chi had built up a successful Chinese takeaway business. I often hung out with him after he'd finished for the evening, having late-night conversations that went on into the early hours of the morning. He also worked long, hard hours and I felt sure he'd enjoy the kind of financial freedom I was striving for. So I told him about the networking group and asked if he'd lend me the £3,500 as an investment, telling him that he would also benefit from the skills and contacts I picked up. He was extremely sceptical; he was convinced it was a scam and he tried to talk me out of it. He said all the usual negative stuff about when something seems too good to be true, it usually is, and how property was not the safe investment people thought it was, that there were huge risks associated with property investment. Eventually, I persuaded him to sponsor me to go on a one-day course that this group held that cost £350. He was more comfortable with this amount.

It was an interesting psychological experiment for me. Of course I could afford the £350 myself, but by having my uncle sponsor me, I made myself accountable to him, too, and that somehow inspired me to work even harder to make the money back. I was more motivated to show him a return on *his* investment than I would have been if it had been my money invested. I was more determined than ever to make it all work. I also had no income stream at that point in time, only the money I'd made on my first property deal, so I felt somewhat vulnerable and wherever I could offset an expense by getting someone else to make the investment in me, I'd jump at the chance.

That one-day course really turned my head. I was surrounded by people talking about property deals, people who were regularly making big profits from doing deals on properties and who were living the life I wanted to live. The more I listened, the more it reaffirmed my commitment. I was soon convinced that I should invest some of my own money.

I joined the group and had a very interesting first year. I partnered up with people—some to a good end, some not. One particular guy screwed me out of a lot of money. He gave me a retainer of £2,000 a month to source deals, but when we made particularly big profits he didn't give me my fair share. It wasn't a nice experience, but I learnt to be choosier about who to go into business with and who to trust.

Uncle Chi was impressed with my success, and when I showed him the figures of some of the deals I'd made, he decided he wanted me to help him invest in property too. It was my chance to repay him for sponsoring me through that initial one-day course. I did a joint venture with him; I found a property in Manchester that was valued at £125,000. We offered £92,000, then borrowed £108,000 against it. Once we'd paid off our loan and costs, we had over £14,000 in our pockets. My uncle got half of that, plus revenue from the monthly rental on the property. I did all the work, but he deserved to share in my success as he was the first person to invest in me, to take a chance on me. He tells me it's the best £350 he ever spent! There's a little jealousy these days from family members who didn't invest in me at the beginning. I've always said if you're not there with me at the start, don't expect to be there with me at the end!

As I got deeper and deeper into the business of property investment, I started to join online forums and other networking groups. I knew I eventually wanted to have my own group and mentor people myself.

One day I came across a group of people criticizing a property investor who had suggested buying properties using lease options. The forum's general opinion was that lease options couldn't be applied to domestic property deals, but this guy was vehemently arguing that lease options were the way forward. He'd made several successful deals using lease options and got them legalized in the UK for the first time. I could see the sense in what he was saying and was eager to learn more, so I contacted him. Little did I know then that that moment marked the beginning of a long and fascinating journey of business and friendship with a certain Mr. Vincent Wong.

* * *

Vince: My first thought when John contacted me was, “There isn’t room in this industry for two Chinamen!” But on this point, I’m happy to say I have been proved wrong. We’re living proof of the notion that two heads are better than one, that 1 plus 1 equals 11. We work so closely and fiercely together that there are times when I almost forget John isn’t my biological brother. This feeling tends to occur both at the best of times and the worst of times! When we disagree with each other, we’re more like brothers than business partners. But we also support each other unconditionally. He’s Uncle John to my kids; he’s family. I guess it’s the similarities in our backgrounds that contribute to our strong bond; and it’s this, along with our shared experiences through the trials and tribulations of building an ever-evolving business, that keeps us going and will sustain our relationship for a long time into the future.

I was born in Liverpool in 1967. My parents, like John’s, had emigrated from Hong Kong. Again, like many Chinese immigrants, they decided their best opportunity lay in the restaurant business, so they opened a place in Liverpool. They were very young when they arrived (only 21) and hadn’t been married long. My elder sister had been born in Hong Kong shortly before they left and they soon had another child (me) on the way. They had very little business experience and were isolated from their families, so they had hardly any support. It was all much harder than they’d expected. They kept going for a few years, but the arrival of a new baby only exacerbated their struggle. In the end, life got so tough that they closed their restaurant and returned to Hong Kong. I was only a few months old. A couple of years later my younger sister was born.

Something about the fact that I was the only child who had been born in the UK, added to the fact that I was the only boy, made everyone treat me very differently from my sisters. I was spoilt, there’s no doubt about that. I was put on a pedestal and worshipped, and no one was more obsessed with me than my mother. She was convinced I was special, that I was going to achieve great things. In Chinese society, favouritism towards the boy is tolerated; it’s more or less expected. I was made to believe I was better than the girls and I felt that people had expectations of me. I was a very cute kid and was constantly told so. Looking back, I'm sure it had quite a negative effect on me. I feel embarrassed when I remember how precocious and arrogant I was at such a young age.

One day my mother saw an advert in the local paper for an open-call audition for child actors. TVB, Asia's biggest TV network, was recruiting young actors and presenters for its children's channel. My mother took my three-year-old sister and me along and we were both offered contracts.

My sister got a few acting roles and received a moderate amount of fame from them, but I was the one who, at the age of seven, took off as the big TV star. I became one of the biggest child actors of the time. I was involved in a whole array of programmes, even presenting some of them; I presented a live show every week. I was very famous within Hong Kong's relatively small community; I used to get spotted everywhere we went and would be followed by adoring fans.

My mother was immensely proud of me. She doted on me. I had far more money spent on me than was spent on my sisters. I got the best clothes, the latest gadgets and all the finest products. I was like a little child doll to her. It must have been hard for my sisters to watch because they were never given as much as I was. But it wasn't as great as it looked from the outside. Yes, I had a lot of fun and possessed many material things, but I craved a normal life at the same time. I was out on the road for long periods of time and sometimes worked long hours. There wasn't a huge amount of playtime. When I did have free time I had far too much money to burn, and by the time I was 12 years old I was a little monster, roaming the streets without supervision and spending money on whatever I wanted for myself and for my friends. For some reason that I cannot even fathom now, we still felt the need to go shoplifting, for kicks. We were terrible; we were like a Hong Kong Brat Pack. I also hung out with many adult friends from work who probably weren't the best influences on me. I remember being involved in some bad crowds. But my mother loved my fame. I was paraded around like a performing monkey, as if she saw my fame as some sort of status symbol. She certainly enjoyed the money I earned. While I'm sure a great deal of it was spent on me, in those days there were not the laws protecting the earnings of child actors that there are today, so I have no idea of exactly how much I earned or where it went.

There is one memory of this time, though, that makes me cringe more than any of the others...my hairstyle. I still can't believe what my mother did to my hair.

Most Chinese boys have the typical straight, jet-black hair. My mother, perhaps wanting me to stand out even further, decided I would have curly hair, so she took me to the hairdressers for a perm. I got a perm when I was only seven years old! I already had fairly light skin compared to the rest of my family. Without the typical Chinese colouring and with a perm on top of that, I stood out a mile. Quite frankly, I looked ridiculous! My dad absolutely hated it. He's a very practical man and he felt it was frivolous and vain. But my mother ignored his protests and took me for regular perms until we left Hong Kong, when I was 12 years old.

My parents' decision to leave Hong Kong was largely based on their desire to give us a British education in the UK. There were two great universities in Hong Kong that were based on the British system, but there was huge competition for places and you needed exceptional grades to get in. My parents felt we would all have a better chance of getting a good higher education if we went back to England and were educated there. My father was also concerned about the changes that might occur in 1997, when Hong Kong would be handed back to the Chinese. I was always going to be a British citizen, having been born in Liverpool, but people born in Hong Kong were unsure where they would stand in terms of citizenship once Hong Kong was no longer a British colony. My father's friend who worked in the immigration office suggested to him that the right to British citizenship, even for those who were born in Hong Kong under British rule, might get complicated. He didn't want to run the risk of being stuck in China.

So in 1979, with Britain on the brink of a historic shift in power led by the first female prime minister (the Conservatives under Margaret Thatcher had just won the general election), we arrived in Wembley. We moved into a new house and I started attending the London Oratory School, a grant-maintained Catholic boys' school in Fulham. My life changed forever. There was no more TV work, no more adoring fans; it was just a regular schoolboy's life. It was a huge adjustment for me. Plus I had to get used to a whole new look in the hair department...because no hairdresser in England would give a 12-year-old boy a perm!

For the first time in my life I really felt—and *knew*—I was different, and not in a good way. I stood out a mile at school because I looked so different from the other boys. It made me feel as if I were somehow ugly and substandard. I became very withdrawn because, like John, I got teased and bullied for being Chinese. I got called racist names and left out of social events. I never had girlfriends like all the other boys did. I had absolutely no confidence and very low self-esteem. It was like I had a complete loss of identity. My early teenage years were probably the lowest time of my life. I was thoroughly depressed.

Life at home only exacerbated my low mood. My father was a bully and an autocrat. He believed in corporal punishment and often physically struck my older sister and me when we had done something he disapproved of. For some reason he never laid a finger on my younger sister; she was exempt from the beatings. By today's standards you would call him abusive, but back then many parents believed it was their right to punish their children with physical force. It was tough to grow up with this style of discipline and difficult to understand what drove him; I think he was trying to curb what he saw as an excessively arrogant attitude in me. What hurt worse than the beatings was the idea that I had let my father down. I craved his acceptance and praise. I felt as if nothing I ever did was good enough. To this day he never tells me he's proud of me; he is as dismissive of me and as negative as he's always been. It's taken me many years, and it's been an uphill struggle, to make peace with his behaviour. In the end, I've put it down to a generational difference of opinion. Whatever I felt, he believed that what he was doing was right and best for us. I know in my heart that he *is* proud of me; he just doesn't know how to show it, so there is no point in staying angry with him. I have accepted him as he is and forgiven him for things he will never apologise for. But I am at peace with my relationship with him. I am simply glad that I have broken the chain because I am a completely different father to my children. I would never punish them physically; I try to praise them and use positive, loving words with them on a daily basis.

In an effort to understand my father better and find excuses for his behaviour, I had to take a good look at his childhood and note how different it was from mine.

My father had a brutal time as a child. His own father was captured and murdered by the Japanese during the Second World War. After this, his mother ran off with another man, leaving my father to be raised by an unaffectionate uncle and aunt who never let him forget that he wasn't their child. His uncle took control of the family business (which involved the import and export of traditional Chinese medicine) that was rightfully my father's, and made him work for a lowly wage. This must have led to years and years of pent-up resentment in my father. Throughout my childhood I remember my parents constantly arguing about money. But they only did it behind closed doors; in public they were adept at saving face—as many Chinese people are—and gave the impression that all was well, no matter what was really going on at home. Again, I swore I would never be like my father in this respect. When I am broke, I tell people I am broke; when I'm doing well, I love to share the good news. I believe excessive pride is dangerous. It's dishonest and dysfunctional to put on too much of a false show; I try to tell the truth, with my head held high, at all times. Lies always lead to problems in the end.

Academically, I did okay up to O levels (what GCSEs used to be called). I had no real social life, so studying was the only option. However, everything changed as we got into the sixth form. While the London Oratory School was primarily a boys' school, it admitted girls in the sixth form. The sudden presence of girls in the classroom had a profound effect on us teenage schoolboys; we all went a little mad, kind of girl-crazed. For me, after years and years of being pushed around and teased, a little attention from one or two girls was all I needed to give my self-esteem a boost. It wasn't long before I was obsessed with girls . . . and my good academic record went out the window!

I completely flunked my A levels, and we were all aware that if I wanted the grades required to get into university I would need to re-sit them. But another year of sixth form was going to be expensive and my parents were struggling financially—and they had already set aside all the money they'd thought they'd need for three sets of school fees. They hadn't budgeted for a rogue son who was going to need to attend another year of school in order to get into university.

Luckily, I ended up being saved by a small, unexpected windfall—which in turn provoked a couple of death threats from other family members!

My paternal grandfather (the one who was captured and murdered by the Japanese during the war) had been married to two women. Polygamy was accepted in rural Chinese society in those days. Because my father's biological mother had run off with another man after her husband was killed, my grandfather's other wife thought of my father as a sort of son—even though she had no hand in raising him—as she didn't have children of her own. Therefore she thought of my father's children as her grandchildren, and, as I was the eldest male child, she left me her estate in her will. She had a fair amount of money invested in property by the time she died. She ignored my father and his brothers, skipping a generation to leave everything to me. The rest of the family was furious and it broke the family apart for a long time, but my father held firm and the money eventually came to me. And it was this money that got me through another year at sixth-form college where I retook my A levels and got the grades to get into university.

I was offered a place at the School of Pharmacy, University of London, and started a degree in pharmacy. It wasn't a subject that particularly interested me, but I thought it would be a good qualification to have, for want of anything else. And in any case, everyone knows that university is more about studying at the so-called college of life than anything else.

Starting university was another massive turning point for me, and this time in a good way. It was my first time living away from my parents (I was in halls of residence in central London), and I had some money left over from my inheritance to burn. The first thing I did (I am ashamed to admit) was to go and get a perm! I even went to Vidal Sassoon for it, which cost me £50—a hefty sum in those days. After a rather miserable time at school, I was ready for a complete transformation and I suppose getting my hair styled in the way it was back in my Hong Kong heyday was symbolic, even if it did still look a little cringe-worthy! I started spending money on clothes and taking girls out. I used tanning beds and ended up with a sort of Latin American look that the girls seemed to love. It was the late 1980s and I was one of Thatcher's children . . . with money. It was a very hedonistic time. I remember staying up all night watching TV instead of studying for exams, thinking, "Oh well, if I fail I will just re-sit the year, which will give me an extra year to party." I was completely irresponsible; I didn't care about the future, I just loved getting attention again. I was lapping it all up. It clearly left some lingering, deep-rooted feelings of guilt because to this day I have recurring nightmares of being in an exam hall with no idea how to answer the questions. I wake up fearful and sweating buckets!

Eventually I accepted that my partying ways had to give way to my studies and I had to start taking my degree a little more seriously. I knuckled down, got to work, and managed to graduate in

1992 with a BPharm(Hons) in Pharmacy. I still had to do a pretraining year to fully qualify as a pharmacist, which I did at a hospital in Surrey. Although the nightlife wasn't a patch on London, I still lived in accommodation with nurses, so my behaviour never became too saintly!

I became a fully qualified pharmacist in 1993, and that's when I knew it was time to grow up and start behaving like an adult. I pledged to take life more seriously. I was still driven by a desire to make my parents proud of me, so I wanted to get a good job, command a decent salary, and build a secure life.

My first job was an interesting one; I got hired by the company that is now known as Lloyds Pharmacy, a community pharmacy started by Allen Lloyd, who was a former employee of Boots the Chemist. Allen's boss at Boots had told him that he was never going to make a good manager. This had enraged Allen, as he was ambitious and determined to succeed, so he quit and started his own rival company. Allen's business model was inspired; he knew Boots had conquered the high street in terms of pharmacies, so he took his shops to the back streets and villages that lacked a local pharmacy. It worked. He initially opened five stores, but with plenty of early success he expanded rapidly. He soon listed on the London Stock Exchange and has never looked back. He successfully proved his old Boots boss wrong!

I threw myself into my work and even took it upon myself to work in my own time, delivering repeat prescriptions to OAPs so that they wouldn't have to make another trip to the pharmacy. My starting salary was £22,000 with overtime, which I was more than happy with at first. But I soon realized, like John did, that whatever you earn is never enough. One of my best friends, Ascanio, had studied at the London School of Economics. While I was out delivering warfarin to octogenarians in Guildford, he was living the high life in London, earning a six-figure salary in the city. I was very jealous and frustrated by the salary ceiling on my job. Eventually I figured out that I could earn more by being a locum, so I chucked in my job and joined an agency, earning between £20 and £25 an hour by travelling around the country working at various pharmacies. The travelling was gruelling and I constantly had to work with people I didn't know, but I earned around £32,000 in my first year as a locum, which I felt justified the extra sweat.

However, *again*, it wasn't long before I was dissatisfied. I wanted to be the best at what I did and I wanted to be paid well for it. But there was only so much I could do in my job. Any additional work, such as my practice of giving the older customers delivery service, was for the most part uncompensated. I felt boxed in again, frustrated and stuck. I was trading all of my time for a very limited amount of money. Something didn't feel right about that scenario.

And then something happened that changed my life again. I guess the epiphany John had as he read *Rich Dad, Poor Dad* was similar to the experience I had as I read a book called *Awaken the Giant Within* by Anthony Robbins. My girlfriend at the time had actually given it to me a year before and it had sat on my shelf for a year. As I grew more and more frustrated with my work, she urged me to read it and finally I did. It completely changed how I viewed the world. I was 26 years old and I knew I wanted to do something more, something incredibly special with my life.

My first thought was that I needed more education, so I enrolled on an MBA course. I was convinced that this would be my ticket to one of those big-shot jobs that Ascanio and other friends of mine were doing in the city. I craved the six-figure salary that I felt sure would allow me to take charge of my life. The fees were hugely expensive and the only way I could fund this MBA was by continuing to work and studying part time. So I made myself available for locum work on Mondays, Wednesdays, Fridays, Saturdays, and Sundays. On Tuesdays and Thursdays I studied during the day and travelled into the Barbican to attend classes in the evening. I needed an initial down payment for the fees, so, like John, I sold my car to pay for my education. My car at the time was a racing green Peugeot 306 with a sunroof, and I got £6,000 for it. I actually cried as the new owners drove it away; I loved that car!

So my life was set for the next two years. I did little else but study and work, believing that the effort was all going to be worth it in the end because my life was going to change forever. I somehow managed to buy a flat during this time as well. Property prices were cheap then, and I found it easy to get a mortgage on my salary. I found a beautiful one-bedroom Victorian conversion with a garden in Clapham North. I bought it for £73,000. I also got engaged to my Welsh girlfriend, Samantha, who had been my area manager when I worked for Lloyds Pharmacy.

I started looking for jobs during the second year of my MBA. I didn't have any immediate bites, but I was sure that the situation would change once I qualified. I was incredibly proud when I finally graduated from business school, the proud holder of an MBA.

My parents even showed up for my graduation, so I knew they were proud of me too. I celebrated by getting married and by selling my flat, which had gone up in value an astonishing £36,000 in one year. Those were the high points of the year; my life was looking pretty good in the summer of 1999. That was just before everything started to crash with such a force that I was left reeling.

First of all, married life was not what I had hoped for. Samantha and I had already been arguing in the months before the wedding, but I'd assumed that this was all to do with stress before the big event. I was sure tempers would settle and our relationship would improve once we were married. I was sorely mistaken. Second, I soon discovered I was no closer to getting a big swanky job despite my new qualifications. In fact, the feedback I was most often hearing was that I was overqualified but underexperienced. I received only one offer in 18 months of job hunting, and the salary was so insanely low I would have had to get a second job just to cover my bills. The final straw came in an interview with a woman who gave me such a dressing-down for having no relevant experience and who was so dismissive of me, telling me that I was delusional thinking I could work for her company in a decent position, that I walked out and swore I would never apply for another job again. I was traumatized. It turned out that what my degree actually stood for was Master of Bugger All.

Eventually, I decided that my only option was to start my own business. I was still pumped up by my MBA, believing it qualified me to earn the big bucks in business. The reality was that it had taught me how to be a good business *manager*, not how to be a good business *owner*, and I was about to learn the hard way what a huge difference there can be between the two.

As the new millennium kicked off—and everyone got used to the fact that the world's computers had not all gone up in smoke because of the Y2K bug—the dot-com bubble was reaching its peak. Inspired by all the über-successful start-ups, such as Last Minute and Yahoo!, I—like so many others—decided I needed to start a dot-com of my own. I thought it would be the perfect start-up business for me since it wouldn't require a huge amount of investment capital. Of course, I hadn't taken into consideration the fact that there was an IT boom taking place hand-in-hand with the dot-com bubble, which meant that web designers and website administrators were able to charge a fortune for their services. To launch my first business, I used all the money I'd made from the sale of my flat, as well as financing I raised from private investors (my parents and most of their friends). I was all fired up; certain that I was months away from becoming a dot-com millionaire.

My website was an Internet dating site...for Asian people. I called it WamBamBoo.com. My brilliant business model relied on there being a huge customer base in mainland China. Because of the unbalanced ratio of men to women in China (a result of the one-child family policy), I imagined this huge untapped market of Chinese men in rural China, all struggling to find dates, all desperate to get on my site and meet women that they could marry. But there was a major flaw in the plan. Sadly, I hadn't considered how underdeveloped the Internet was in China. A huge majority of these men in the rural parts of China didn't even have computers, let alone access to the Internet. It was a disaster. I knew I still had a market outside China, but my largest customer base didn't have access to the site. I felt a complete fool. But rather than admit defeat, I continued to pump money into the company—maintaining a staff base, running servers, and paying for marketing campaigns—until eventually I physically couldn't keep it going anymore and I had to close it down with losses of over £300,000.

As it was a limited company and all the money had been invested as shares, I didn't have to pay anyone back, but I had just lost all the money my parents and their friends had invested. Failure of any kind is not tolerated in Chinese culture, and people will do anything to save face. My father was deeply disappointed in me. Everything I had done was against his wishes. Not only had I let him down personally, but I had also let down his friends. He was understandably furious.

As my business started to fail so did my marriage. Less than 18 months after we got married, Samantha and I separated. She had never supported my website idea, and while she had helped to support us financially, she never supported my aspirations. We were always struggling to agree on anything and it was something of a relief when we finally admitted defeat and ended our marriage. I moved into a dingy one-bedroom flat in Wandsworth where I licked my wounds and continued to watch my business go downhill. It was in that flat that I experienced some of the very darkest days of my life, and if I hadn't met the love of my life I dread to think how far off the rails I might have gone.

Newly single, with a failing business, I was forced to go back and work as a locum, which obviously made me even more miserable. I also started trawling the Internet for dates and went out with a series of attractive women. I never invested much in any of these women; I just needed them to stroke my heavily bruised ego. Eventually, I woke up to how shallow I was being and started focusing on personality rather than looks. One day, about a year or so after my marriage had ended, I struck up an online conversation with a Danish woman called Annika. I was intrigued that she had not posted a picture, but I soon didn't care what she looked like because she had such a beautiful spirit. She was kind, loving, and straightforward; she also seemed very genuine in comparison to some of the women I'd met online. We got along so well that we were soon chatting every day. I stopped looking at any other profiles. Then the day came when we were due to meet and I don't think I'd ever been so nervous. I'll never forget the first moment I saw her face—she was literally the most beautiful woman I'd ever set eyes on and I knew I'd found her: the woman I wanted to spend the rest of my life with. That first amazing weekend we spent together confirmed this feeling.

We didn't have an easy start to our relationship; we were under a lot of pressure. Annika had recently moved back to Denmark to start a nursing qualification. The weekend we met in person she was just visiting London to pick up some things she'd left with friends. I knew it was going to get serious from the moment I saw her. We'd already become very close online and over the phone. I couldn't let her get away. I considered moving to Denmark, but I had too many ties to London, responsibilities I couldn't turn my back on. Somehow I managed to persuade Annika to move back to London to be with me. Luckily her feelings were as strong as mine. I could only imagine her parents' horror as they stood at the airport seeing off their 25-year-old daughter who had quit her nursing degree to go back to London to live with a not-quite-divorced 35-year-old Chinaman with a debt-riddled, failing business whom she'd met online only a few months earlier! I was overwhelmed by her faith in me, and six weeks after she moved to London to be with me I proposed. Within six months we were married, and the following year our beautiful daughter, Hannah, was born.

Having a wife and child to support was exactly the motivation I needed to get out of my depression and rebuild my life. It literally saved me. I could let my father down, I could let myself down, but there was no way I could ever let my wife and child down. I set about with more determination than ever, brainstorming ideas for a profitable business.

Finally, two clues from my past experiences came together and gave me my eureka moment.

I started thinking about the big chunk of money I'd made on my Clapham flat; it was the only time in my life I'd made serious money. I was struck by how much money could be made from property. Then my thoughts turned to the Internet marketing skills I'd developed while building my website. A dating site for Asian people might not have been the right business to market, but I knew I had the skills and experience to run a successful marketing campaign. I put these two ideas together and came up with the idea of building a web site for property sellers and investors. I could see that a database full of leads to good property deals would potentially be extremely valuable. I could help find investors for people who were motivated to sell their properties quickly. And that's how Network Property Buyers—my property-networking website—came into being.

I started with relatively little capital this time and hired a developer in Ukraine to build my website, NetworkPropertyBuyers.co.uk. Many business owners hire offshore IT people these days, but back then only a few people had cottoned on to how cost effective it could be. My database of property leads was launched and grew exponentially. It was extremely successful from the get-go, and I made a real name for myself as someone who could generate genuine, useful leads; someone who knew how to find motivated sellers. I started buying a lot of property myself, and my reputation grew as I came up with more and more inventive ways of financing deals. Eventually I found I was being sought after for my opinion. I was asked to speak at conferences and seminars, and was even interviewed by the BBC.

Some of my ideas were a little unorthodox, for example, my idea to apply lease options to buying domestic property. I received a lot of resistance to this particular idea, but I stood my ground and eventually got lease options for domestic property legalized. Even more people started to contact me after that, but I couldn't talk to everyone; I only had so much time. One guy was particularly persistent. I kept telling him I was too busy to meet with him, but he didn't give up. Even when he played the Chinese card it didn't sway me…at first!

Finally John wore me down and I agreed to meet. He just wouldn't take no for an answer (and in that respect he hasn't changed much!). Like many people who were interested in gaining exclusive access to my list, John wanted to go into business with me, but rather than paying for leads, he wanted to give me a cut of the deals. I'd heard it all before. Many people had approached me with similar offers. For the most part I'd been disappointed. At best these people usually did nothing; at worst they made deals behind my back and then disappeared without paying me my share, leaving me to chase them and subsequently get screwed over if I couldn't track them down. John kept assuring me that he was different, that he was completely trustworthy. He also told me that as he was becoming an expert at closing deals and I was becoming an expert at lead generation, he was sure we could be a formidable team. Even though I was still wary, there was something about John's passion and tenacity that persuaded me to take a chance on him.

John impressed me from the outset. He was good to his word. I could see how hard he worked, and this led to excellent results. Every Friday, without fail, his personal assistant e-mailed me a spreadsheet of all the leads he'd contacted and the deals he was negotiating. I got a cheque for every deal that I was due a share of as soon as it went through. It's rare to find someone so honest and trustworthy in any business, and something told me this was a relationship worth investing in. I was soon convinced that this was a guy I could be in business with long term.

It wasn't long before I had more than a business partnership with John. We became firm friends and shared many stories of our ups and downs in life, which made us feel even more connected. One of the first things that struck me was how John and I were both motivated by our fathers... but by the desire to ensure that we did *not* become like them! We had both grown up watching our fathers be dogmatic and small-minded in their beliefs. They had both taught us that life was about trading your time for money and that it was frivolous to think of doing otherwise. They took the safest roads possible, they did not tolerate failure, and they took no risks. But John and I didn't see that this approach made our fathers happy... so we were inspired to do the opposite.

My partnership with John grew rapidly, getting stronger all the time, and one day he approached me with a new business idea. He wanted to package our extensive knowledge and offer it to others as an educational course on property investment. As we had more than a decade of experience between us and were experts in our own niches, he felt that we had a huge amount of valuable information to offer. It seemed like a great idea, and one that would generate another income stream. We did our research and couldn't find anyone else teaching exactly what we were planning to offer: namely lead generation, alternative financing options, and deal making. There was definitely a gap in the market for what we could teach. Ostensibly, yes, we would be teaching people to compete with us, but we couldn't buy every property out there! There's always room for more property investors. We could help them fast track their businesses by encouraging them to learn from the mistakes *we'd* made. In fact, in the wake of the global financial crisis and the bursting of the property bubble, there were more motivated sellers than ever, in desperate need of offloading their properties or relieving themselves of their mortgage commitments. We were both thoroughly inspired and excited at the prospect of teaching and helping others to become financially free like us. And thus Wealth Dragons was born.

While it was John's initial idea that kick-started the business, I take credit for the name, which has proved to be more meaningful than I even realized at the time. We were brainstorming a name for the company and John came up with Property Dragons. When we researched it we found that the name had already been taken, and in any case, I believed we were teaching people more than simply how to profit from property deals: we were teaching them about the importance of passive income and financial freedom. The slight alteration to Wealth Dragons that I came up with has made all the difference and is even more relevant today as it so perfectly defines what we do. We agreed on that name, and the rest, as they say, is history.

* * *

John: I'd never worked harder in my life than in those first few months when we were setting up Wealth Dragons and starting to recruit students into our seminars and courses. Everything was riding on it; our necks were on the line and we both had to sacrifice a lot of time with our friends and families. This was harder for Vince, as he was married with a young daughter; he was sacrificing precious time with her. I was terrified of failing, but after teaching only a few seminars I knew we were on the right track. As a former aspiring actor (one of my dreams before I got into animation), being on the stage was electrifying for me. As our audiences got bigger and my confidence grew, I knew I wanted to expand and take our company global. One day I got a call from a huge promoter of motivational speakers, who was offering Wealth Dragons a major international tour starting in Asia . . . the following week!

* * *

Vince: I will never forget the day I got a call from John in the middle of the night telling me we had to leave for Asia the following week. At first he was so excited I could barely make out what he was saying. When I finally got the facts out of him, I said it was impossible. Annika, Hannah and I were about to leave for the South of France. We'd hired a villa for a month and were going away for some much-needed rest. I'd been working too hard and felt I had neglected my family. I needed to make it up to them and we all needed to spend some quality time together. John kept insisting that this Asian tour would be the making of us. In the end I agreed to run it past Annika, but I told John that she would have the final word. She considered all the facts carefully and said that I should go. Obviously we lost a lot of money cancelling the holiday, but what I gained professionally, and eventually financially, more than made up for it. Plus, Annika and Hannah joined me for part of the tour and we were able to spend time with my older sister, who lives in Singapore.

Heading out on what was to be a six-month tour was a huge risk and meant a great deal of sacrifice, but it paid off. It was the making of Wealth Dragons in that it established John and I as leaders in property-investment education and introduced us to an international audience. But perhaps more importantly, it reaffirmed my wife's unshakeable and unconditional support for my endeavours, which brought us even closer together and strengthened our already happy marriage. And that, in the end, will always be the most important thing for me.

> He who has a why to live can bear almost any how.
>
> —Friedrich Nietzsche

PART I

THE WHY

The first part of this book looks at *why* you want to be wealthy as well as what we call your *moral obligation* to become as wealthy as you can. People are often surprised when we say this but we honestly believe that you have a duty to become as wealthy as possible. The only thing that stops people from achieving everything they are capable of is *fear.* We have a whole chapter on fear in Part II, so before we discuss what fuels our fears in depth and examine all the excuses you make for why you can't or shouldn't create limitless wealth, let's look at all the reasons why you *can* . . . and *should.*

CHAPTER 1

What Is Wealth?

When I was young I thought that money was the most important thing in life.
Now that I am old, I know that it is.

—Oscar Wilde

Before we determine what the definition of wealth *is*, let's discuss what it definitely *isn't*. Monetary wealth is not a pile of cash sitting in a bank account. Even if you have money in a savings account, the amount you earn in interest is not likely to be anything to get wildly excited about. And if you find the need to dip into it to supplement your monthly outgoings, and you're not constantly topping it up, it will be depleted very quickly.

No, cash in the bank is the very last thing that makes us *wealthy*.

So is your wealth simply whatever you own in assets? Well, only those that are appreciable assets, such as your house, your art collection and your business (potentially) should be counted. But you still have to subtract your liabilities to come up with a figure that is your net worth.

What is your net worth?

Write down the value of all your assets (everything you *own*), then write down the total amount of all your liabilities (everything you *owe*). The difference between these figures is your net worth.

Your Assets – Your Debts = Your Net Worth

Many people think they are wealthy because they have a big bank balance and some equity in a property, but when they subtract their mortgage, their car loans, their credit cards and other debts, they realize that they are effectively broke.

Don't get depressed if you have a negative net worth at the moment. You may technically be "worthless" at the moment, but there is plenty you can do (as you will discover by the time you finish reading this book) to change that. Also, many people live in a state of negative worth. We've been sucked into a culture of carrying debt; we are the second generation of "have it all now, pay for it later." Our grandparents would be horrified at how much debt we get into these days!

But there is another way, a better way, to live. There is a way of massively increasing your net worth. You can see it if you just look at the equation above. All you need to do is increase your assets and reduce your debts. The more *appreciable* assets you have, the easier this becomes.

So monetary wealth is a fairly straightforward measurement. But that is only one type of wealth that we are talking about here. We also place a huge value on what you are worth to the world in terms of your attitude and feelings. We are talking about your *moral wealth.*

How can we really define and measure moral wealth?

While we all have slightly different values and beliefs, there is a general code of ethics that most of us try to live by. Abiding by the law and not stealing or harming others is obviously the basic level of a moral code. Beyond this, the level at which individuals show compassion and generosity towards others, the depth of their integrity (honesty, trustworthiness, and reliability), and any other attributes they possess, and actions they take that contribute to enriching humanity, are all factors that count towards determining how morally wealthy they are.

This is great news for people who realize they are technically worthless in monetary terms. At least they can feel wealthy in some respect! In fact, increasing their moral wealth is the way some people contend with having little monetary wealth. However, the more you increase your moral wealth, the more you should be inspired to increase your monetary wealth, so that you can literally *do* more with your great moral wealth!

These two types of wealth—monetary wealth and moral wealth—are very much related, even though they appear very different and tend to produce different feelings in people. High moral wealth generally makes people feel positive and good about their purpose in the world. High monetary wealth makes people feel empowered. So it follows that a person with high moral wealth should want high monetary wealth in order to do more good in the world.

We will come on to explore the relationship between monetary and moral wealth more closely in the next chapter. The point is, people can be monetarily wealthy, and they can be morally wealthy; the two are technically independent of each other, even though they can have a strong relationship. Of course, conversely, people can be monetarily worthless and/or morally worthless.

When people have low or negative moral wealth, this can lead to immoral behaviour. This may cause them to want to harm others, and even sometimes themselves. The most dangerous type of person is one with negative moral wealth and high monetary wealth. Money often gives these people ways of covering their tracks and enables them to pay for expert legal defence to get them off serious charges. After a highly publicized and televised civil trial, O. J. Simpson was acquitted of murder. In a private lawsuit he was later held accountable for damages relating to the wrongful deaths of his victims, suggesting that the evidence against him pointed to his guilt. He is now in prison for a totally different crime; he is serving 33 years for robbery. The point is, how was he acquitted in one trial and found guilty in another? Presumably it had something to do with his ability to pay for some of the best and most expensive defence lawyers. A person of more limited means might have had a different outcome because he or she wouldn't have had such a good defence team. And what about the case of Dominique Strauss-Kahn, the former head of the International Monetary Fund, who was accused of sexually assaulting a chambermaid in a hotel in New York? He was acquitted of the charges. Would a different man, a less high-profile man, with limited means and a weaker legal team, also have been acquitted? It's interesting to ask these questions.

It seems that it does not necessarily follow that high monetary wealth *leads* to high moral wealth.

Neither does high moral wealth necessarily lead to high monetary wealth.

In their day, great artists and literary figures such as Van Gogh and Shakespeare were often broke. They had high intangible value because they were so talented and were producing works of art. But these works did not become extremely valuable until after their creators' deaths. When they were alive these people had high moral wealth but low monetary wealth—although one could easily argue that Van Gogh's moral wealth was questionable because he caused himself great physical harm in cutting off his own ear. He was quite possibly depressed or suffering from some form of mental illness. Perhaps he was unaware of his talents. Perhaps if someone had helped him raise his self-worth, his moral wealth, he may have gone out and sold more paintings and become a monetarily wealthier person. J. K. Rowling clearly had enough self-worth to believe she had something of value when she submitted her Harry Potter series to publishers. Despite being repeatedly turned down, she never gave up. Now she has monetary wealth (intellectual property is a highly valuable asset, often appreciable and also generating income from royalties and licenses) and we have the wealth of her Harry Potter stories. Imagine if she had buried them in a suitcase and died before they were ever discovered . . . both she—and the world for a certain length of time—would have been deprived of a great deal of wealth!

CHAPTER 2

The Moral Obligation to Be Wealthy

You were born to win, but to be a winner you must plan to win, prepare to win, and expect to win.

—Zig Ziglar

Ultimately, what we are trying to do here is take a holistic approach to what we traditionally call wealth. As we've said, it's certainly not all about money in the bank. Monetary wealth is very much dependent on assets, and moral wealth is largely about what we offer back to the world in terms of good deeds and compassion—what we can give of ourselves to those in need, and whether we give physically, financially, or both.

So which is more important . . . monetary wealth or moral wealth?

Initially, you might assume the answer to that question is moral wealth; that high moral wealth is the ultimate goal, because without it monetary wealth is too easily put to bad use. But without monetary wealth, the difference a person with high moral wealth can make in the world is limited. If you have high morality and good intentions but lack the power to put your goodness to positive use, and you don't have the means to contribute to worthy causes, the power of your moral wealth is somewhat limited—or even diminished—in its capacity to be of value to others.

Let's examine this relationship between monetary and moral wealth more closely.

If you have high moral wealth, you can't necessarily translate it into high monetary wealth. You could try your best to sell your art or spread your message and monetize your work but you might not be able to make any tangible gains from it. In fact, a lack of monetary wealth can easily erode the high moral wealth of people if they became trapped in poverty and are unable to help themselves, let alone help others. A real dearth of monetary wealth can make the most upstanding and loving person bitter and resentful. If times get particularly tough and people feel trapped by poverty or debt, they may even lower their moral standards in their desperation to get out of the trenches.

By comparison, if you have high monetary wealth you automatically have a choice. You can choose to have low moral wealth and keep your fortune to yourself, to spend on frivolous—or even dubious—activities, or you can use your money to enrich your life and the lives of others. You can actually invest in *increasing* your moral wealth. You can *pay* to spread your message; you can *invest* in your art or in helping others with theirs.

Bill Gates has reportedly said that when he dies his children will only inherit $10 million each . . . despite the fact that he gives more than that amount away to charity every year. He said he wants his children to make their own way in the world, although he notes they are fortunate in getting a massive head start. Gates and Warren Buffett have both said that it is their aim to have given away most of their fortunes (at the end of 2013 reported to be around $76 billion and $58 billion, respectively) before they die.

A very touching story unfolded in Los Angeles in 2005 when *Los Angeles Times* journalist Steve Lopez came across an extremely talented musician playing the cello in downtown Los Angeles. The man was homeless and in pretty bad shape. Lopez helped the man rebuild his life and it turned out he was a Juilliard-trained cellist called Nathaniel Ayers who had suffered a mental breakdown, which had led to him developing schizophrenia. If you watch the film or read the book (*The Soloist*), you will see how in helping Ayers, Lopez was also forced to battle some of his own demons and how the whole experience improved his own life.

Money solves the problems that *not* having money creates.

It would appear that acquiring monetary wealth is actually extremely important, and this is why we are suggesting that you have a *moral obligation* to become as wealthy as possible, and that *not* increasing your monetary wealth as much as you can is potentially damaging, and even irresponsible.

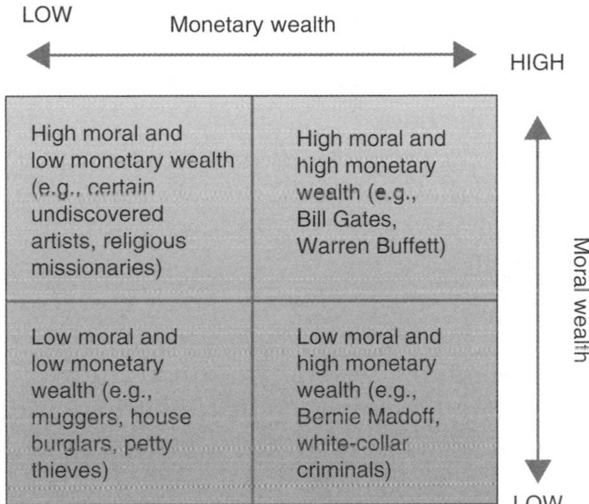

Figure 2.1 A Pictorial View of the Relationship between Moral and Monetary Wealth

Now it's clear to see why the box we should all be aiming for in Figure 2.1 is in the top right-hand corner. Many people assume that they have done enough if they sit in the top left box—that as long as they have high moral wealth, they are doing everything they can for themselves and humankind. But this really is only half of the ideal scenario. What is the point of sitting around *wanting* to give a lot of money to good causes if you have no money to give?

Vince: *I have people who tell me that they are put off the idea of making money because rich people seem to do bad things. I point out that the number of rich people they have heard such stories about—due to the fact that their bad deeds have made national headlines—are a tiny fraction of the seriously wealthy, financially independent people in the world. There are plenty of incredibly wealthy people, doing extremely good things and leading happy lives, who are not splashing their actions across the front pages of newspapers. Saying that rich people are all bad because money makes some people do bad things is like saying anyone with a moustache is a mass murderer because Adolf Hitler and Saddam Hussein had moustaches.*

You should always be striving for more monetary wealth in order to spread your moral wealth further afield, to put it to ever more good use. The strange sentiment that many people seem to have is the assumption that as they increase their monetary wealth their moral wealth will decrease. This is absolutely related to the warped view that the desire for money is synonymous with greed . . . greed being an undesirable trait, of course. We will come back to this false assumption later in the book.

For all the reasons we've discussed in this chapter we strongly believe that the top right-hand box should *always* be the ultimate goal and that having high monetary wealth as well as high moral wealth should be what we all strive for.

Would the world really be a worse place if everyone had a lot more money? More money simply provides more choices. If good people make more money, which gives them more choices, surely that's preferable than the limited choices they have without money. If you are a good person, is it not your *responsibility* to make as much money as you can?

CHAPTER 3

Why a Wealth Dragon?

Nearly all men can stand adversity, but if you want to test a man's character, give him power.

—Abraham Lincoln

Money is power. No one can deny that. If you have money you have the power to be able to *do* more, *see* more, *learn* more, *own* more, and *give* more than if you don't have money. So if you don't have a clear idea of what it is you want to do, see, learn, own, and give, then you probably haven't been too focused on making the money to obtain that power.

What comes first, though: the money or the power? We believe it's the power. We're not born financially wealthy (most of us aren't, anyway), but we believe that we *are* all born with a huge amount of potential power.

Our goal is to teach people that this unleashed power lies within them; it lies within all of us. We want to help people understand *why* it is so important to tap into that power and then *how* to harness it in order to achieve whatever they want. What exactly they do with it once they have taken hold of it is a choice everyone must make for themselves.

People often ask us about the significance of the word *dragon* in our company name—why we called our company Wealth *Dragons* and why we talk about teaching people to *become* wealth dragons.

There is a very strong message associated with the image of the dragon. Essentially, a dragon is a mythical creature that has been used for centuries to symbolize different things according to the culture and context. In England, the dragon is traditionally seen as a dangerous thing that must be destroyed. The very heart of England's heritage is steeped in dragon folklore. For generations English children have been taught the story of St. George, the patron saint of England, who slays the dragon. Interestingly, some of the earliest versions of the story suggest that the dragon was infected by a plague and that this was the reason George killed it, not because it was a dragon *per se*.

England's neighbour, Wales, uses the dragon as one of its national emblems. The Welsh dragon—specifically, a *red* dragon—appears on the Welsh flag and is synonymous with all things traditionally Welsh. The colour of the dragon is particularly important because it comes from the legend that the Welsh *red* dragon defended an invasion from an English *white* dragon.

So it seems that dragons are not so terrible, as long as they're on your side. There are good dragons and bad dragons. And sometimes there are dragons infected with a plague that must be slain by brave saints!

Dragons appear consistently and prominently in Chinese culture too. The dragon is a national symbol of wealth and good fortune in China; it is a very powerful symbol. As such, it is also a creature associated with royalty and deities. Historically, the Chinese have believed that the ruling dynasties were intrinsically linked to God, and that the ruler had a divine mandate that could only be challenged if he failed to rule the people well. That, in itself, was a tall order. Because the ruler was believed to have unlimited power and to be on first-name terms with God, he was believed to be responsible for everything that happened. So even if there was a spate of natural disasters, wiping out crop harvests and destroying properties, the emperor could be blamed and a rebellion justified.

The dragon symbolizing Chinese royalty is no ordinary dragon due to the fact that it has an extra claw. The five-clawed dragon is highly revered in China. The emperor always had a five-clawed dragon on his yellow robes, and if you ever see a dragon with five claws depicted on an object—say, a piece of art or furniture—it means that it was probably once owned by a Chinese emperor. Yellow was also an auspicious colour that only the emperor was allowed to wear. Anyone else found wearing yellow was executed.

In the Chinese calendar the dragon is the luckiest, highest-ranking animal. Every 12 years there is a big baby boom in China, with people trying to have children born in the lucky Year of the Dragon (the most recent being 2012).

Chinese dragons do not breathe fire, but they do fly, and they are large and powerful creatures. This suggests that the dragon can both *do* harm and *protect* from harm, depending on how it chooses to use its power.

The same is true of people who become *wealth dragons*: Depending on how they choose to use their monetary power, they can do great good or great harm.

For us, one of the greatest Chinese dragons was Bruce Lee. His Chinese screen name, Li Xiaolong, literally means *little dragon.*

John: *The story of Bruce Lee really resonates with me. He was born in the year and at the* hour *of the dragon in San Francisco, the son of a leading Chinese actor. Although he was born in the United States his family returned to Hong Kong (at the time a British colony, but under Japanese control for three years during the Second World War), and Lee dedicated his life to studying martial arts. He eventually returned to the United States and succeeded in breaking down many stereotypes surrounding Chinese people and the practice of martial arts. I appreciate the message he conveyed: Fighting skills are not necessarily a bad thing if they are not put to bad use, they are simply part of a person's discipline and power. He pushed himself to the limit and, sadly, died at the young age of 32, but his story is still inspirational. If you've never seen it, I highly recommend watching the film* Dragon: The Bruce Lee Story *with Jason Scott Lee in the leading role.*

Vince: *There's a scene in that movie that I love, in which Jason Scott Lee, as Bruce Lee, is travelling to the United States from China and gets chatting with another Chinese man. He tells this guy it's his ambition to become one of the greatest Hollywood actors—to be a trailblazer for future Chinese actors and to set a precedent of Chinese actors taking leading roles and not simply being typecast. This guy is a history teacher, but he tells Bruce Lee that he has no ambition to work as a teacher once he gets to the United States. He says Chinese people would only ever get jobs as construction workers or be given work by other members of the Chinese community who own the many Chinese takeaways. The history teacher assures Bruce Lee that he doesn't have a "Chinaman's chance" of making it in the United States. The expression is* *one that is widely used even today, to indicate that a person has only a very slim chance of achieving something.*

We also identify with the characteristics of a dragon. A dragon is brave, strong, and aggressive: all the qualities that are required of a *wealth dragon.*

Courage is what separates the winners from the losers. You need courage to face your fears and go through the pain barrier, to get outside of your comfort zone. Courage enables you to take action, again and again, even after you've failed spectacularly.

Strength is what you need to keep you going when the going gets tough. Again, winners are strong. Weak people are quitters. It takes real strength to keep getting up every time you get knocked down, to face up to whatever has beaten you in the past, to believe that *this* time you will win. Mental *and* physical strength are required. To keep your body and mind as strong as possible, you must eat well, exercise, and get enough sleep. Forget the stories you hear about famous people operating on three or four hours of sleep a night: You can't make good decisions when you are tired, and you need your rest in order to stay healthy and to be able to operate at your best.

Aggression is not often viewed as an attractive quality, especially in the West, but in the martial arts it is the aggressive spirit that produces the right moves. The most aggressive animals rule the animal kingdom, and the same is true of the human world. Aggressive does not mean destructive, it simply means one who dares, wins. If you want to win you must be aggressive. You can still dress up your aggressive stance in charming and polite outer packaging!

So that explains the *dragon* part of our name.

As we explained in our introduction, it was a stroke of luck that we ended up calling our company *Wealth* Dragons rather than *Property* Dragons, especially now that the education we offer has gone far beyond teaching people about property investment. We quickly discovered that most people need more than some courses in property investment in order to become wealthy. It became clear that most people who came to us needed to reexamine their whole outlook and attitude towards money. We believe we may be the only organization in the world that teaches a programme combining property investment with self-development, life skills, and personal growth! As our seminars took off we were amazed to discover how much time we were spending with people unravelling years of conditioning and dispelling long-held beliefs, such as the belief that the accumulation of wealth is tantamount to greed (greed being regarded as a very bad thing). We were shocked to find out how many people had extremely negative associations with money.

So we also found that it was not enough simply to *educate* people. We needed to help *motivate* them too: We had to help them find a big enough *why* to get wealthy before showing them *how* to do it.

The people who come to our seminars are from all walks of life, but they all have something in common: They've been running on a treadmill they didn't even realize they'd got onto and they don't know how to get off—they can't seem to find the emergency stop button. We just show them where it is and give them permission to press it.

If there's one thing we want everyone to come out of our seminars believing, it's this: Making money is relatively simple. There's plenty out there and it isn't too hard to find. Once you find it, it's well within most people's capabilities to get it, in a perfectly legitimate and ethical way. What's hard is for people to believe—really, truly believe—that they are entitled to go and get it.

A determined, strong, courageous, and *active* dedication to creating and building wealth is what makes a person a *wealth dragon*.

CHAPTER 4

Undesirable Truths

There is nothing either good or bad, but thinking makes it so.
—William Shakespeare, *Hamlet*, Act 2, Scene 2

Consider everything you hold to be the truth right now. How much of it is set in stone as hard facts and how much of it is your BS (belief system!)?

Obviously, you can't change things like the time and place of your birth or your genetic makeup, but after that, there are so few limitations. Can you change your sex? Yes. Can you change your name? Yes. Can you change your nationality? Yes. Such changes may not always be easy to accomplish, but they are all achievable if you really set your mind and heart on the outcome.

There is so much that you can do, no matter what you currently think. As Henry Ford said, "Whether you think you can or you think you can't, you're probably right." The first step to achieving anything is to *believe* you can do it.

Where do our thoughts and beliefs come from? Most of us were raised with a barrage of so-called facts that were thrown at us on a daily basis, almost from birth. If we never challenge those alleged facts, we are living in other people's shoes, believing other people's truths and not carving out our own path in life. You may challenge something you were raised to believe and find that you agree with it. That's fine ... as long as you've questioned it and reached your own independent conclusion.

One purported fact the majority of us have been told repeatedly from a young age is that a good education will guarantee you a good job and a secure future. It might be a good idea to tell young children this in order to help them understand why it's important to go to school, but it is a bit of a false promise in that there are no *guarantees.* The statistics don't support this so-called fact. Every year highly qualified graduates pour into an already flooded job market and end up unemployed or in menial jobs, and every year we hear more rags-to-riches stories of successful, rich entrepreneurs who dropped out of school at 16.

Quickly think of the names of the wealthiest, most successful Brits.

Which names first came to mind? We find many people, when asked this question, think of Richard Branson and Alan Sugar. Neither of them has a university degree. In fact, both men left school at 16 (Branson with a very poor academic record on account of his dyslexia).

There is a big emphasis put on getting a formal education these days, but a really good education, like charity (as we are going to talk about later), should begin at home. Children need to be taught core values and good behaviour, and about world issues, by their parents first and teachers second. But many people seem to assume that a good education can replace good parenting. Do we inherit this kind of thinking? If our parents weren't taught by their parents to think outside of the box and to challenge old beliefs, then how are we going to know any better?

Most of us, when we first went to our parents and asked for money, were told to get a job. We were told that if we wanted to have money we had to go and work for someone and get paid for our labour. Few of us were told to go and open a business, or were given a small sum of money and told to invest it wisely and let it grow. We were given pocket money in exchange for doing chores, and later encouraged to go and get a job that would pay us a set wage for a set amount of hours given in labour.

Vince: *I was raised by my parents to believe that a good formal education, with lots of academic qualifications, was the key to success. But as soon as I got my MBA, which is considered a particularly prestigious qualification, I was repeatedly told that I couldn't get the jobs I wanted because I was overqualified without relevant experience. My brother-in-law had the same problem. He* *couldn't get a decent job anywhere in the UK, even with a PhD. He and my sister ended up moving their family to Singapore, where he was able to secure a decent research post. Plenty of graduates from British universities end up working in menial jobs. Can you imagine how depressed and disillusioned these young graduates feel? They've spent three years studying and shelled out a fortune on their education, leaving them drowning in debt, and then they end up flipping burgers and frying nuggets . . . if they're lucky. A high number of recent graduates remain unemployed.*

We're not saying that a formal education *can't* secure you a good job, but it certainly doesn't give you any *guarantees*. We feel young people should at least be told that there are more options, paths to success other than sticking it out in a formal educational programme that doesn't necessarily suit them. What is the real value of a spoon-fed education? Even if you do get a good job with your great grades, you are not immune from redundancy and you are still being paid a set salary in exchange for giving up most of your time.

A formal educationmay make you a living, but self-education could make you a fortune!

Throughout this book, we're going to be suggesting a number of what we call *undesirable truths* that challenge opinions that seem to be widely held. We call each suggestion an *undesirable* truth because people would rather believe the alternative—the myth that we're attempting to debunk. They actually feel safer trapped in their old BS, spouting out all the excuses as to why they do and don't do certain things. If they accepted the undesirable truth, they'd have to *change*!

Here's the first undesirable truth that we want to share with you.

The Truth about Education

We've been told:

People with the best grades get the best jobs.

The undesirable truth is:

Self-education creates the best opportunities.

From a very young age, we're told to stay in school and work hard in order to get a well-paid job. What we're not told is that while you're getting your formal academic qualifications, others are getting the experience that will put them ahead of you in the running for the job you want. If you enjoy studying, by all

(continued)

means do it. If you want letters after your name for learning a whole load of stuff that you read in textbooks written by other professional academics, great. There is absolutely nothing wrong with getting a formal education and studying a topic that you are passionate about. Some jobs obviously require certain qualifications. You can't be a doctor or a lawyer or an engineer unless you get the required qualifications. But even when you qualify you are not guaranteed employment for the rest of your life, and don't kid yourself that an MA in ancient history is going to guarantee you a career of any kind. If you don't like school, if you find studying in a formal way difficult (perhaps because you have dyslexia or a limited attention span), then *leave* and find something that you *do* love and get a job doing that. Then work your way up through the ranks until you know enough to start your own business, doing the thing you love. Perhaps eventually you'll end up training others to do what you do, and then you'll be able to sit back while your beloved business makes a healthy profit and brings in a passive income for you. There are so many different paths to a successful career... *a formal education is only one of them and comes with no guarantees.*

Vince: *I wanted my daughter to learn about profit and loss as soon as possible. I didn't know anything about profit and loss until I was 27 and had spent a lot of money on going to business school, after which I still lost a huge sum of money on my first business venture. So at nine years old, my daughter, Hannah, started her own business buying and selling organic eggs. She found out there was a van delivering these beautiful organic eggs that stopped near her school. She bought a few half-dozen boxes of eggs for 80p and sold them to people in my office for £1.50. After a couple of trial runs I taught her to take orders and money up front, so that she was never out of pocket or buying more eggs than she could sell (we seemed to be eating a few too many omelettes at the weekends, made from unsold eggs!). The business was popular, and eventually she made a deal with the delivery guy to come to the office (saving her dad's petrol bill!). She was soon making around £30 a week. When Uncle John comes to visit, he always quizzes her on her business strategies, and I love to listen to them talking about unique business propositions and profit margins. I am extremely proud of her... and tell her so regularly.*

Whenever we ask people in seminars if they were educated about money and personal finances at school, most of them look at us blankly. Why don't they teach us about money at school? Why aren't we encouraged, even as children, to learn about business? Why do we tell our children to put their money in a piggy bank? As far as we know, pink ceramic pigs offer a grand total of 0 percent interest on your savings!

Here is another undesirable truth.

The Truth about Saving

We've been told:

Save money for a rainy day.

The undesirable truth is:

Invest money carefully so there is enough for all days (regardless of the weather!).

The mentality of saving for the future, of storing money away for a rainy day, is just more scarcity thinking. It's an attitude that breeds fear. Tucking money away in an account where it is earning a small amount of interest, rather than investing it in something that returns a regular income stream, is ultimately wasteful. Money in the bank is not working to its best potential for you. Obviously it is wiser to save some money rather than spend every penny you earn immediately, but saving is certainly not the key to financial independence. The first rule of investment is diversification. A good money manager will advise you to split your money four ways: some is left in the bank for spending, some is invested in appreciable assets like property, some is invested in a good portfolio of stocks and shares, and a small amount is what we'll call gambling money—for investing in opportunities with higher risk.

When we first started to offer people an education in property investment we discovered that this was actually not the best place to start. We thought we just needed to share our knowledge and that it would be enough to allow people to follow in our footsteps, but we soon discovered that there was so much more to educating people than simply showing them the best way to invest in property. The majority of people we met had such a warped, skewed attitude towards wealth, and were carrying around so many false ideas about money, that we had to start from much further back and re-educate them on how to think about money.

One of the biggest myths that people seemed to believe was the inverse relationship between money and happiness. Whoever started this rumour was a very poor person, in terms of both cash and spirit.

The Truth about Money

We've been told:

Money doesn't buy you happiness.

The undesirable truth is:

Money doesn't guarantee you happiness, but it can enrich your life and the lives of those you love.

Money can't protect you from bad things: Tragedy can strike anyone's life at any time. But while things are going well and your life is where you want it to be, money can certainly contribute to your happiness. Nobody with a healthy net worth who is able to spend quality time with the people he or she loves would tell you otherwise. It is not the money *per se* that makes such a person happy—but money makes the lives of these people, and the lives of those they love, more enjoyable. People who say "Money doesn't buy you happiness" are usually those who have prioritized making money at the expense of investing in other areas of their lives. It's sour grapes on their part. They failed, so they want to pull you down with them; they are bitter. If you completely sacrifice all the things that make you happy in pursuit of money, then, of course, money will make you unhappy. But that's not the point of making money. You are not making money simply for the sake of making money: You are making money so that you can enrich your life. If money enables you to do the things you love—such as travelling to new cities and taking part in specific activities and sports (skiing, sailing, and so on)—if money allows you to do things that make you happy, then—make no mistake about it—money can, indeed, buy you happiness.

> I have all the money I will ever need . . . if I die by four o'clock.
>
> —Henny Youngman

CHAPTER 5

Welcome to the Parallel Universe

It does not do to dwell on dreams and forget to live.
—J. K. Rowling, *Harry Potter and the Philosopher's Stone*

In the film *The Matrix*, Morpheus, the character played by Laurence Fishburne, is trying to explain to Neo, played by Keanu Reeves, that the world he has been living in is a virtual world, where everything is programmed and controlled by machines. Morpheus wants to show him that the real world is a very different place. But first Morpheus needs to teach him to reject what he's been programmed to accept: that his virtual world is just "the world that has been pulled over your eyes to blind you from the truth." Did the Wachowski brothers intend this to be a metaphor for the world we live in?

There's the world we are programmed to believe in by the powers that be, and then there is a very different world we could live in if we're prepared to shake off the blinkers. In this real world we have far more choices than we previously thought we had. Many people find it very hard to reject the world they have grown accustomed to living in and to challenge what they've been taught; they'd rather live blindly. Some people live happily like this. Well, we want to expose a parallel universe, where so much more is possible, to those who are unhappy with what they think they have to accept as reality.

But just as Morpheus tells Neo, we can only show you the door—*you* have to walk through it.

The Value of Embracing Failure

One of the biggest misconceptions about entrepreneurs is the assumption that their success is always dependent on starting from an advantageous position. A popular belief is that most successful people had a serious leg up: They must have had money to burn or some kind of sponsorship, or they were born with silver spoons in their mouths. In most cases nothing could be further from the truth. Some have had help, no doubt, but many have risked everything to get where they are today. The only difference between a successful entrepreneur and someone who gave up after a setback is simply that the unsuccessful person gave up. It's important to fail, and to keep failing, on your way to success. But you haven't ultimately failed until you quit. *Successful people simply don't quit!*

> **In your universe:**
> *Failure is frowned upon; you are taught to avoid failure and to be ashamed of it.*
> **In the parallel universe:**
> *Successful people embrace failure because they know that no one has ever been truly successful without failing plenty of times.*

We have had as many failures and setbacks as the next person. We've lost money, lost friends, and had many strokes of bad luck; we've dealt with all kinds of problems. But when problems arise, we deal with them; we don't run away.

Vince: *I'm a successful entrepreneur . . . most days! But I didn't get where I am today without some bad days (some of them very bad indeed). The only difference between me and the person who has not been successful (so far) is that I kept going. The day I closed my Internet business, with losses of over £300,000, it would have been fair to call me spectacularly unsuccessful. But I picked myself up and started another business, which ended up being a huge success. It's swings and roundabouts. You win some; you lose some. I have my bad days to deal with even now, but the difference between me now and me back then, or between me and another entrepreneur, is that I deal with issues calmly, appropriately, and with conviction. I don't panic; I simply get on with it.*

The Truth about Failing

We've been told:
It's bad to fail.
The undesirable truth is:
Failure is an essential step on the path to success.

In his book *Adapt: Why Success Always Starts with Failure*, British economist Tim Harford exposes the myth that we can protect ourselves from failure by arming ourselves with enough knowledge. Experience counts for far more, and that means experiencing failures as well as achievements. Furthermore, the world has become an increasingly volatile place. What worked once is not necessarily relevant now. We can't rely on the old systems and structure that were once perceived to be infallible. We have to learn how to survive when our banks collapse, when our businesses fold, and when personal tragedy strikes. We must fail in order to learn valuable lessons. Failure should be celebrated. Without failure, we wouldn't have many of the inventions that our modern lives depend on. We've all heard the stories about Thomas Edison failing thousands of times before inventing the light bulb, Colonel Sanders being turned down over 900 times before he succeeded in selling his fried chicken recipe, and *Gone with the Wind* being turned down by almost every publisher. If we want to be successful, we have to be prepared to fail. We should embrace failure because it is a necessary step towards success.

Apply the value of failing to entire nations. Look at Germany and Japan, the countries that lost World War II. Today they are both massively successful economies. Yes, they failed, but they came back stronger. The strong German motto *Nie wieder Krieg* (never again war) drives a pacifistic country that has only strengthened as a result of its purported failures. Conversely, Britain does *not* consider itself to have failed. Because Britain thinks it won most of its battles (carefully writing history books to play down the atrocities committed in the name of colonialism, for example) it seems it doesn't feel it has anything to learn. Think of Britain and Germany in terms of two people: one who always wins and doesn't feel he has anything new to learn, and one who has failed many times and keeps reinventing herself and learning new strategies for success. Which do you consider the most successful? Statistically, it is Germany. In December 2013, the (British) Centre for Economics and Business

Research optimistically announced its prediction that Britain's economy will surpass Germany's in the year 2028. We remain sceptical.

The Learning Curve

One of the reasons so many people don't succeed is that they get off the learning curve just before it starts to produce results. They start out along a path, have some ups and downs, learn a little, make slow progress—and then, just as they are about to make a big leap forward, they quit. Then they get onto a new, different path and start the whole process again—again quitting as they get to the really hard part.

Unfortunately, most people have never looked at or studied a learning curve. If they had, they would see that there is a long, long interval with very little progress. At a certain point, after what seems like almost too long to keep going, there is a sharp incline in the curve and progress starts to snowball exponentially.

Far too many people get off a learning curve just before that critical upturn. They jump onto a new learning curve. When that one also doesn't produce the results they want, they jump to another one. They keep jumping. It's as if they're running around in circles getting nowhere. We've all known someone who's done this. Most of us have *been* that someone! If you want to succeed, you can't be fickle. You have to stick to one learning curve and keep going, accepting

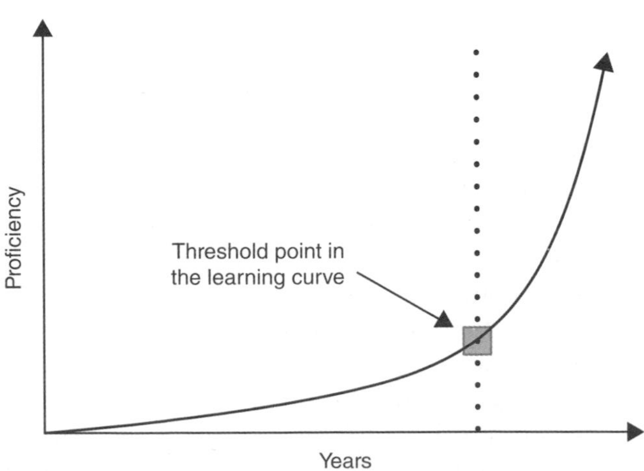

Figure 5.1 The Learning Curve

that obstacles and pitfalls are essential parts of the learning curve. After all, as the old saying goes: Experience is what we get when we don't get what we want!

In *Outliers*, Malcolm Gladwell suggests that it takes 10,000 hours to become an expert at something—that it is not simply innate talent that gets people to the top of their game; it is hard work and relentless practice. Too many people give up just after they reach 9,000 hours without getting the success they wanted. As Bruce Lee said, "I fear not the man who has practiced 10,000 kicks once, but I fear the man who has practiced one kick 10,000 times."

In your universe:
When you don't succeed on your chosen path after a while, you are advised to change it.

In the parallel universe:
You stick to your path, go through the pain barrier, and get onto the accelerated section of the learning curve!

Vince: *I know what it's like to go through that pain barrier of the learning curve. I really believed it couldn't get worse after I had to shut down my first business with such huge losses. In hindsight it was an experience I needed to go through, because I used all my mistakes to teach me how to do things differently in my next business, which turned out to be incredibly successful. With all the experience I have now I think I could make a success of almost any business. I believe I could go down to a market tomorrow, open a fruit and vegetable stall, and outsell any of my competitors. I believe I could do this because I have learnt, through years of trial and error, the best business practices. I often suggest to my students that they go and watch a fruit and veg seller in action. Go down to a local market and watch them sell. The successful ones make a huge fortune. It's a lucrative business, and a great one to learn in. Alan Sugar started out working for a greengrocer! Business is business. Sugar says it's simple: Buy low, sell high. It's when people start to complicate that process and deviate from it that they tend to fail. If you've lost focus, go back to basics; go watch the market stall owners. It's like in the movie* Rocky III *when Apollo Creed tells Rocky he's lost his edge; he takes Rocky back to basics at his old gym, where he sees young fighters who are hungry for success, with the "eye of the tiger" in their expressions.*

In the parallel universe, you have to get out of your comfort zone. No longer is life about doing as you're told, living under someone else's umbrella of security. You have to get wet, get dirty, get hurt, and ultimately survive all hardships in order to reap the rewards of your efforts. What others regard as humiliation we regard as the building blocks of success. We welcome failure because we know we will learn from it. We don't want security; we want risk. Only by taking risks can we grow. Growth brings us results that lead to rewards.

When there is stagnation, there is no growth, no results, and no rewards.

Sun Tzu, the ancient Chinese general who is credited with writing *The Art of War*—a book that has become popular reading not only for military strategists, but for political leaders and business managers—advises army generals to throw their troops into dangerous situations. "Confront them with annihilation, and they will then survive; plunge them into a deadly situation, and they will then live. When people fall into danger, they are then able to strive for victory."

John: *There's a saying in Chinese culture: "If you want to learn to swim, you can't sit in the boat. You must break the boat. Then you will* have *to swim to survive." To learn and really move forward, you have to put yourself in risky situations and figure out how to survive. People come to us and want us to show them how to achieve the good life, but they say they're uncomfortable with selling. You have to do the hard work, the work you don't like, to get where you want to be. It applies to anything. If you want to get fit, you have to start running or going to the gym. If you say, "I want to make a lot of money but I don't like selling," you may as well say, "I want to get fit but I don't like exercising so I'm not going to do it." You can sit around wishing for it but it's not going to happen overnight. You are not suddenly going to wake up fit because you've wished for it. If the government could persuade people that there was a fitness lottery that you could buy tickets for, and that you would be instantly fit and good looking if you won . . . now there's a business idea! Perhaps the publishers of weight-loss books are thinking along these lines. Most people read endlessly about losing weight without taking any action.*

You can't learn to drive by reading a book. You have to go out and do it!

Living in the parallel universe—the real world—is tougher than living in the one you've been used to (as Neo discovered in *The Matrix*). It's far less attractive, tastes less appetizing and is filled with many more dangers than the one that's been designed for you . . . but it is *real*.

You Don't Have to Be Bad to Be Rich!

Here's another myth that people love to put around: All rich people are mean, greedy, selfish people just waiting to cheat you out of your hard-earned cash because, of course, that's the only way you can get rich . . . by making others suffer.

For the most part, this could not be further from the truth.

One of the most successful and benevolent foundations in the world (indeed it is the world's largest foundation) is the Bill & Melinda Gates Foundation. Bill Gates has ploughed billions of his own money into a nonprofit organization dedicated to improving the lives of people facing poverty and disease; people who, without the efforts of the foundation, would struggle to survive. What motivated Steve Jobs was not money; it was a passion for computers, and his belief that they could change and improve the world we live in. Jobs believed computers and humans could have a more symbiotic relationship, and he worked tirelessly towards that goal. Mark Zuckerberg was driven by the idea of people connecting through cyberspace. His commitment to keep expanding and developing Facebook may have earned him huge sums of money, but people who know him report that Zuckerberg has always lived a quite simple and modest life.

In your universe:
Rich people are mean and corrupt.
In the parallel universe:
Most rich people are kind and philanthropic.

Not everyone who is rich is a flashy, greedy swine. This is a fallacy mostly put about by people who resent the fact that they do not have money themselves. Granted, the wealthy people we are talking about tend to be the ones who are self-made: People who suddenly come into money when they haven't worked for it, through an inheritance or winning the lottery, often don't know how to appreciate or manage their wealth. And of course there are always those few people who are financially wealthy but morally poor, who end up putting their money to bad use. But for the most part, the wealthy people we've come into contact with—especially those who are self-made—seem to be extremely good people with honourable motives who enjoy giving back to the community and helping less fortunate people. You just don't often hear about most of them because they don't tend to make the front pages of the tabloids!

John: *The thing I love most about having money is the freedom it gives me to help people randomly. I've always appreciated good service and excellent quality, so when I had one of the best meals I've ever tasted in the back streets of a small town in Malaysia, I left a £50 tip, even though the meal itself had cost around £2! The chef came running after me, worried that I'd left my money behind (proving what a good, honest person he was). When I told him I'd left it for him, he almost cried. Another time, when I was visiting San Francisco, I saw an old Chinese guy busking, playing the violin. He played beautifully and he reminded me of my grandfather. It really touched me and I stood listening to him for ages. Before I walked away I left $100 in his case. He was stunned. But why shouldn't I do that? I appreciated the guy's music and I had the ability to give him that money, so why not do it? I have loads of little stories like these. Another one of my favourites happened while I was in Taiwan and saw a guy in a market selling gum. He had no arms or legs. But he was proud. He wasn't begging; he was selling gum for a profit. I tried to give him $200, but he refused to accept it. He only wanted to sell me gum. So I bought all the gum for $200 and started giving it away. That $200 probably fed the guy for months. You can't feed everyone in the world, but you can feed a lot more people when you're rich than you can when you're poor. So if you have the opportunity to be rich (and if you're reading this book, you do), why wouldn't you take it?*

We love the story of the richest man in Asia, Li Ka-shing (and not just because his name is so amusingly close to ka-ching!). He built his empire from nothing. He was born in China to a modest family and was forced to leave school at 15 and get a job to help support the family when his father died. He moved to Hong Kong as a refugee with nothing and managed to get a job working for a plastics company. He was putting in endless hours to earn a living, but he also absorbed as much knowledge as he could. Eventually he was able to open his own successful plastics company and started investing in Hong Kong real estate. He went on to invest in property, banking, telecommunications and steel production, as well as many other businesses throughout Asia. He is famously philanthropic, donating huge sums of money to charity every year whilst maintaining a relatively modest lifestyle.

But even Li Ka-shing is constantly subject to negative comment and criticism in the media. We've come to believe that you haven't really made it, that you are not truly successful, until the Internet is awash with people slating you!

Of course there's always going to be people who put their money to bad use, but money is only a tool. If you give someone a gun, would he use it to protect himself or to harm people? Money doesn't change who you are. In fact, if anything, money only *accentuates* the person you are. If you are a generous person, you can be *more* generous with money. If you are a destructive person, you will be *more* destructive with money—which is why, sadly, we see some famous rich people destroying their lives with expensive drugs. There are just as many—many more, in fact—who don't!

In your universe:
Money changes people for the worse.
In the parallel universe:
Money doesn't change you; it magnifies you.

If you were an awful person before you had money, you'll be an even worse one once you have money. If you were a generous person (perhaps only able to be generous with your time and your compassion) before you had money, you'll be able to do much more for others once you're wealthy.

Getting and Spending Money

The other message that comes from the Li Ka-shing story is that anyone can make money. Contrary to popular belief, it's simply not true that you have to have a lot of money to make a lot of money. Who's putting this story about? Possibly the same ones telling you that rich people are all greedy and selfish, and that money doesn't buy you happiness. Li Ka-shing started with absolutely nothing. He worked hard to earn money to invest in his own business.

Vince: *I know people believe that you need money to make money, but it's simply not true. You need to figure out how to get the initial money you need, but it doesn't have to be your own. I got investors for my first business.*

It failed. I found the money for my next business a different way. You need to be resourceful. *If I lost everything tomorrow, the last thing I would do is panic. I would simply start figuring out how I could make money again—how I could build my business back up. I would hatch a plan; I would make it happen.*

In your universe:
You need a lot of money to make a lot of money.
In the parallel universe:
If you are really serious about your business and you believe in yourself, you will find the money to build it.

If you are committed, creative, determined and courageous, you will find the money to invest in your business. But don't expect anyone else to believe in you until you believe in yourself. If you're struggling to get investors for your business, look in the mirror and ask yourself whether *you* would invest in *you*. Be honest. If the answer's no, work on the issues, fix them, and ask again. Repeat the process until the answer is yes. Only then will you start to find the investors you want.

You do eventually have to start spending your own money to make money. Money is fluid. If you hold onto it, never letting any go out, you won't find much coming back to you. If you spend a little, maybe you'll find a little comes back. When you start investing a lot of money in your business—*and* in yourself—you'll find a great deal of it comes back to you.

In your universe:
Spending money on yourself is indulgent... that is, a bad thing.
In the parallel universe:
You treat yourself as you treat others... generously!

There's a real propensity towards frugality in Britain, a suggestion that it is somehow wrong and frivolous to spend money on treating yourself to nice things. You need to get out of that mindset as soon as possible.

Sadly, we've discovered that when we spend money on ourselves and our families we seem to encounter a lot of criticism (mostly from people who don't know us very well). People judge us simply for enjoying the fruits of our labours. It's a strange attitude, and possibly one that is, again, motivated by jealousy.

People think that rich people forget the value of money…but that's exactly what they don't do. They might enjoy spending it, but they never forget the value of it.

John: *One summer I decided to take my whole family on an all-expenses-paid luxury holiday to the United States. I flew them to Florida first class and put them up in a five-star hotel. We ate at the finest restaurants, took part in all the exciting activities and saw all the sights. I spent just over £30,000 and it was worth every penny to see the enjoyment they got out of it. The flip side was the attitude of people outside of the family who showed jealousy or made judgmental comments. Some people have this false perception that I have forgotten the value of money. I recently complained to a so-called friend about being quoted £8,000 for car insurance (it was a very expensive car!). His attitude was flippant; he said it didn't matter because I could afford it, that it was no hardship. It was difficult for me to point out that £8,000 is still a lot of money for car insurance and that you don't stop looking for value just because you can afford something.*

The Truth about Frugality

We've been told:

Frugality is a virtue.

The undesirable truth is:

Frugality defies the natural direction of the universe. The universe is always expanding; if we don't expand with it, we are working against it.

There is always more money. When you truly embrace this fact you will never need to or want to be frugal again. The happiest people we know are those with an abundant mindset. Actually, it doesn't matter how much money they have: Their mindset is independent from their net worth. We know wealthy people with an abundant mindset, and we know not-so-wealthy people with an abundant mindset. We also know wealthy people with a miserly mindset, and of course less wealthy people with that attitude too. The point is, it doesn't matter how much money you have; what matters is your attitude towards that money. If

(continued)

your attitude is to hoard it and never spend it because you fear it is finite and you might not get more of it, you have a miserly mindset. If you think of it as easily replenished, you are thinking with an abundant mindset. There is always more. Generosity is a virtue, and that means being generous towards yourself as well as others. The more you give, the more you receive.

Vince: *One of the worst cons of recent times is the way people have been brainwashed into thinking that there is no money around during a recession. There is plenty of money around in a recession. A recession is simply a slowdown in economic activity on a macroeconomic scale. But business owners use a recession as an excuse to make cutbacks and carry out redundancies that will line their own pockets. In actual fact, for investors a recession is a great time to make money. It's a time to buy property as prices slump and a time to play the stock market because it becomes particularly volatile. Smart traders made a fortune shorting the banks during the financial crash of 2007–2008. How do you think the government can afford to bail out the banks if there is no money around? There is plenty of money. There will always be plenty of money. There is no shortage of money. If you want it, all you need to do is learn how to make it, and keep making it, in all economic climates!*

John: *I have this great analogy about the difference between abundance thinking and scarcity thinking. There are these tribes in the jungle who catch monkeys by putting nuts into small holes in trees. A monkey puts its hand in, grabs the nuts and then tries to get its hand out. But it can't because it has made a fist in order to hold the nuts and it can't get the fist back through the hole. It's stuck and the tribe catches it. If only it had let go of the nuts, it would have been able to run free. If I hadn't let go of that initial £10,000 that I paid to Ying Tan to help me get started in property investment, I wouldn't be where I am now.*

What's the Limit to What You Can Achieve?

Steve Jobs had what his coworkers called a *reality distortion field.* He would ask a developer how long it would take to perfect a certain product or piece of software, and if she said 18 months he'd tell her to do it in 2. And he always got what he wanted. He knew no bounds, no limits. He used his charm and persuasion to *distort the reality* of the developer's mind so that she stopped looking at the reasons why it would take so long and started to believe she could do it in two months. It worked. This strategy played a large part in Steve Jobs's success. He was a perpetual optimist. When it came to business, he didn't take no for an answer. It all comes down to what you believe is possible. Steve believed it would take 2 months; the engineer believed it would take 18. But Steve said do it in 2 months, so that's what she had to do . . . if she wanted to keep her job with Jobs!

In your universe:
There's a limit to what you can achieve.
In the parallel universe:
The only limits are those you impose upon yourself.

While you are still living and breathing, you can always reach for more and push your limits beyond what you thought was possible. Really, if you don't, what's the point of living? If you're not always striving to make improvements in your life and better yourself, if you're not looking for something new—an interesting challenge, a goal, a test of what you once believed to be impossible—then you're not really living life for all it has to offer . . . you are just existing.

Living in Excuseville

We seem to live in a society suffering from a crippling epidemic of procrastination. If we had a penny for every time we've heard "I'm not ready to go for it just yet" or "The timing's not quite right for me to do this" or "I'm just waiting until this happens before I really go for it" we'd be worth double our net worth! People will always put off today what they say they will do tomorrow . . . mostly because they are scared. What it would take most people around six months to do we try to get done in a couple of days. That's how you succeed. That's how you get ahead of the pack. You have to be prepared to do things in a fraction of the time another person would take. That's all Steve Jobs did: He got there first.

Most people live in a land called Excuseville. They constantly come up with reasons for why they can't achieve something. They love coming up with these reasons because doing so justifies why they haven't got what they want. They could never say "I'm scared to go for it" or "I'm too lazy to do what it takes"—they will simply come up with reasons such as "I'm too old now and the competition's too great" or "I don't have the time; I've got three young children and a demanding job."

In your universe:
You have a whole list of excuses why you can't have what you want.
In the parallel universe:
You are stronger than your excuses.

Look at how much Stephen Hawking does with nothing more than the ability to move a couple of facial muscles. Consider Nick Vujicic, a motivational speaker who was born without arms or legs. When I hear people moaning about their problems and complaining about their lives, I always reference Hawking and Vujicic. If these guys can achieve what they've achieved, then so can you!

Taking Action

There has been a flood—a flood on a biblical scale—of self-help and law-of-attraction books that advocate visualizing what you want. These books really get under our skin and frustrate us because they often only offer half the answer. Yes, it's important to visualize your goals and know precisely what they are, but you are never going to get rich by writing out imaginary cheques for a million pounds or get a sports car simply by pinning a picture of it over your bed!

Many of these books don't even begin to suggest a game plan that lays out how readers are supposed to get the money for their coveted yachts or their dream houses by the beach. There is absolutely no way you will get these things simply by wishing for them. That's delusional; that's one step *below* buying lottery tickets!

A lottery ticket is not a business idea or a retirement plan, and neither is a visualization board!

Obviously there is an important place for the concept of the law of attraction in helping us realize our dreams; we do need to *believe* that we will achieve our goals. We must adopt an *abundant* mindset or we will never get there mentally, but we will only physically get there by putting in the hard work, making a plan and following it through. If it helps to pin a cheque for a million pounds above your desk, go ahead, but understand that it is nothing more than a motivational tool: You *still* have to put in the hard (sometimes uncomfortably so) work to achieve what you want.

Successful people do not have hopes and wishes; they have targets. They set themselves goals and then do whatever it takes to achieve them. If they fail one way they try another; they adjust their methods until they get there.

In the parallel universe we are pragmatic. We say, "What do I have to do to get what I want?"

In your universe:
You hope and pray for your life to change. You don't take responsibility for what happens to you.

In the parallel universe:
You make a plan to make changes in your life. You take charge of everything within your control (which is usually more than you think!).

It's not easy. Of course it's not easy. If it were easy, everyone would be loaded and living the high life. Most people give up at the first hurdle or the first sign of hardship. These people have negative attitudes. There is always a payoff and hardships are part of the process. If you think of all the difficult things you have to overcome to get somewhere, if you have a negative outlook, you'll never get anywhere. If you know you need to go to the gym but your thought process goes something like "Oh no, I've got to go to the gym, so I've got to find all my gym clothes, then I've got to get the car out and drive all the way there, then I've got to find a parking spot, pay for the parking, walk over to the gym, get changed, and find a free machine before I can start my workout," you're never going to leave the house. If you can teach yourself to do all these things on autopilot while you keep thinking about that amazing endorphin rush you're going to feel shortly after working out, it's going to make you get up and go.

Most people don't have the self-control to be accountable to themselves. This may be one of the reasons that highly educated people don't always do as well as people who learnt the ropes by working from an early age. If you've been spoon-fed an education, you may expect to be told what to do all the way through life, so working for an employer, with limits on your working hours in exchange for limits on your earnings, is probably best for you. But if you are a rebel, a high school dropout or someone who always thinks outside of the box and challenges the rules, you could put all that initiative to good use, start your own business and eventually become very successful!

Your life will not change until you take **action**.

Sometimes we feel like we are fighting an epidemic of apathy that is reinforced by the government urging everyone to buy lottery tickets. The very existence of the lottery encourages apathy. Why do we have adverts pushing people to buy tickets and to believe in the dream of winning a million pounds so that they don't have to work for the rest of their lives? Why don't we see the same number of adverts encouraging people to invest in appreciable assets or to build a profitable business?

People are not inherently lazy; they are inherently in denial about the length of their existence. We procrastinate because we think there will always be more time. We put off today what we could do tomorrow because we *assume* tomorrow will always come. If you knew you had two months to live, you would start living your life very differently. When Steve Jobs was told he only had a couple of months to live, he worked harder than ever because he wanted to leave a legacy. He planned a whole range of products that would continue to be rolled out long after his death. We haven't even seen half of them yet!

The Truth about Your Time

We've been told:

There's a finite amount of money and an infinite amount of time.

The undesirable truth is:

There's a finite amount of time and an infinite amount of money!

It is imperative that we let go of this false notion that we have an infinite amount of time with only a finite amount of money. If you run out of money, you can easily make more. When you run out of time, that's it: You're dead. Our mortality is something most of us won't face, but it's the most definite thing there is. (As the old proverb goes, nothing is certain but death and taxes.) We cannot create more time, turn back time, or live forever, so we should do as much as we possibly can with the time we have while we have it.

Anthony Robbins suggests that there are only two conditions that prompt people to take dramatic action: they are either greatly *inspired* or they are completely *desperate*. We say: **get inspired before you get desperate**!

Define the **why** strongly enough to get you out of your comfort zone and get you properly motivated. If you have two arms and two legs, and live in a free country, you should feel an *obligation* to get up and do everything you can with whatever you have.

Our greatest wish is to inspire you to make a plan to build a fortune. At the very least, even if you don't follow through with that, we hope we're giving you a manifesto on getting really *honest* with yourself. If you are not being honest with yourself, you cannot move forward. If you are giving yourself *reasons* for why you are not achieving what you want to achieve, *reasons* for why you are not happy, *reasons* for why you can't do something right now, and *reasons* for why all the things you need in order to succeed are out of your control, then you are living in a *badly* distorted reality.

When you have the guts to own up to the fact that the only *reason* you are not doing something is because you won't, then you can wake up to a whole new reality: a parallel universe where everything you want is suddenly within your reach. When you take *full responsibility* for where are you in life, you can become infinitely powerful.

Once you realize that *your* work—the work you do when you invest in yourself and your own business—is actually going to get you the results you want (instead of simply fulfilling the requirements of your boss or the company you are working for), it doesn't feel like work anymore because it's a real investment in your future.

In your universe:
You work because you have to.
In the parallel universe:
You work because you want to.

The parallel universe does not seem an attractive place at first. It looks like it is full of huge hurdles and uncomfortable obstacles; it looks like a lot of hard work. But the rewards are so much greater than those on offer in the universe you are in—and they are limitless.

The harder the battle, the sweeter the victory.

> Remembering that I'll be dead soon is the most important tool I have ever encountered to help me make the big choices in life. Because almost everything—all external expectations, all pride, all fear of embarrassment or failure—these things just fall away in the face of death, leaving only what is truly important. Remembering that you are going to die is the best way I know to avoid the trap of thinking you have something to lose. You are already naked. There is no reason not to follow your heart.
>
> —Steve Jobs

PART II

THE WHEN

If someone offered to give you a million pounds with no strings attached and said, "Do you want this now or next year?" what would you say? You'd want it now, right? Well, technically that million is on offer to you all the time if you're prepared to work for it. So when do you want to start to work for it, now or next year? If the answer is not *now*, then you may need to fix some of your thinking. In this section we are going to look at some of the obstacles that stand in your way and stop you from reaching for your goals. Once you've removed those obstacles, you're free to start working on the *how* to become... *infinitely wealthy*!

Get Rich Quick or Get Rich Forever?

There are people who have money and people who are rich.

—Coco Chanel

Do an Internet search for get-rich-quick schemes. If you check out every search result, you'll probably be sitting at your computer for the best part of a month. The world is awash with people convinced that they have the answer to getting rich quick. What they are suggesting is not so much getting rich quick as getting rich without doing any hard work: getting rich lazily without any guarantees. For the most part, this is an enticement to get people to register (and sometimes pay a lot of money up front). In our opinion and experience, getting rich takes a great deal of hard work, and it doesn't happen overnight.

One of the biggest perpetrators of promoting a get-rich-quick scheme, of manipulating people into thinking it's easy to become a millionaire without doing any work, is the UK government.

Every day, on every commercial channel, you see adverts for the lottery. Huge billboards advertise the lottery. Tickets are available everywhere. People are lured into gambling every time they stop for a newspaper or a cold drink. Most of the lottery adverts are specifically designed to encourage people with modest lifestyles and limited means to part with their money in exchange for the unrealistic expectation of winning millions . . . without having to work for it. Nowhere in the advertising is there a responsible warning that says:

> *WARNING:* The odds of winning the jackpot are around 14 million to one; you are 305 times *more* likely to be struck by lightning.

Vince: *It used to break my heart when I worked in pharmacies and watched people with very little money come in and buy lottery tickets; buy hope. They'd all been sold a false dream by the government. The responsible thing to do would be to teach them how to* **earn** *a million, not convince them that they are one ticket, one pound, away from* **winning** *a million. These people are convinced that the lottery is their only hope of being rich, but that is not true. Everyone has the chance of making a million if they are prepared to do the work. Millions of people, every week, spend their hard-earned money on buying lottery tickets without even being fully aware of how ridiculous the odds are. And these are not people with money to spare. I used to deliver prescriptions to pensioners who would eat cold dinners because they could afford either to heat the house or to cook their food . . . not both.*

The government is making a fortune from these people, who in turn are unable to heat their houses. There are people who actually believe that the £1 they have in their pockets is better spent on the outside chance of winning some money on a lottery that would change their lives than on a few hours of heat. And no one is doing anything to convince them otherwise. One pound spent on false hope rather than a hot meal—it's sad.

There are people who collect their unemployment cheques and go straight to the newsagents to buy their lottery tickets. These people are being made to believe that the answer to their problems is gambling. If these people wanted to invest in a business and get a financial education, they would be frowned upon and told they don't have the right attributes. They are led to believe they are worthless, that their only chance of having a good life lies in six numbers written on a piece of paper that gives them a 14-million-to-one chance of winning a fortune.

Every day people are spending their money on scratch cards and lottery tickets, believing that this is their quickest way to amass a fortune. Luck is being sold to us as a false sense of security. In our opinion, there are a number of epidemics gripping this country—namely, laziness, procrastination and apathy. Add gambling to that list!

Someone who has spent £10 a week on lottery tickets and scratch cards for the past five years has spent £2,600 on predominantly worthless pieces of paper. Isn't that nuts? They might have won £10 three or four times. Even if they've won ten times (and they probably consider themselves lucky if they have), that's £100. So they've still wasted £2,500. They've spent £2,500 on absolutely nothing but the unrealistic dream of winning a few million. They could have invested that money in an education. Why didn't they think they were worth investing in? Why do they think they are worth less than a few scraps of paper and card? Even if they'd saved the money in a high interest account they'd have a guaranteed return in excess of the amount they won on the lottery, as well as their initial capital investment. They didn't actually win at all; they suffered a significant loss.

As the government's adverts tell us, "You've got to be in it to win it." How about, you've got to be insane to be in it!

We have people who walk into our seminars expecting to be able to press a button and watch money fall from the sky (perhaps largely thanks to those lottery marketing campaigns!). We often say at the start, "If you are looking for a get-rich-quick scheme you won't find one here, so you have our permission to leave now with a full refund." Those who stay often come back to us months later and tell us we have transformed their lives.

Aside from the familiar joke about robbing a bank, there are no guaranteed (legal!) get-rich-quick plans anywhere. If getting rich were easy and quick everyone would do it; it takes hard work and a long time to build wealth.

If you see something advertised as a get-rich-quick scheme or if someone is promising to make you a millionaire overnight, be very wary. The one thing we emphasise again and again and again to people who attend our seminars and become our students is the length of *time* it takes to build wealth. It takes time and *action.* Our hearts sink when we see enthusiasm turn to inaction. People sometimes invest in our training, get all fired up in the room, and then go away and do nothing.

The one thing we always promise is to show people *how* to build wealth. That doesn't mean everyone wants to do it or *likes* doing it!

No matter how many times we say things like "This is not a get-rich-*quick* plan," "You will have to be braver and take more risks than you ever thought possible," and "You can't have the baby without the pain," we get people coming back to us moaning that building wealth is taking too long or that it's too difficult to get off the ground.

And this is what we hope sets ours apart from many other this-is-how-you-get-rich books. We will always tell *the truth* about how hard it is to build real wealth. It's always possible, but it's always hard work.

Who Is Stopping You?

Family and Friends: Fans or Foes?

An insincere and evil friend is more to be feared than a wild beast; a wild beast will wound your body, but an evil friend will wound your mind.

—The Buddha

As we discussed earlier, a huge amount of what you believe about life has been handed down to you by your family. Your perspective will be greatly determined by the company you keep, by the people you hang around with. That's not to say that you will agree with everything your family and friends say, but the influences of people we love leave deep impressions on our psyches. Mental conditioning is a powerful tool. Our thought processes determine how we behave, the decisions we make, and even what we think of ourselves. If those thought processes have been heavily influenced by negative people, then even if we strive to be positive and work hard at self-development it can be a long uphill climb to rid ourselves of destructive thought patterns.

Vince: *I had to overcome a lot of negativity that had been passed down to me by my family. I always felt as if nothing I did was good enough for my father. Even when I started making a lot of money, instead of telling me I'd done well, he attributed it to my good fortune in marrying a lucky wife! I'll never forget the most hurtful thing he ever said to me. He was sick, and as a* *trained pharmacist I tried to give him advice. He said, "Why should I listen to you; you're not a doctor. If I need advice I'll go to a doctor." It was dismissive and hurtful. If a stranger had said this to me I wouldn't have cared. But it was my father. His words cut deep.*

Negative people are very powerful. They love saying things like "I told you so" when things don't go well, and they can easily make you give up on your goals. And because (as we know) things rarely *do* go well on our first attempts, these people have plenty of supposed evidence to back up their negativity!

The Truth about Your Friends

We've been told:

Your friends have your best interests at heart.

The undesirable truth is:

Everyone has his or her own best interests at heart; therefore, so should you!

You have your group of closest friends, the people you hang out with all the time. But take a step back once in a while and take a good look at them. Are they always encouraging you to do new things, to learn, to build, and to move forward? Or do they usually rain on your parade, coming up with reasons for why you shouldn't do the things you suggest? We call these negative naysayers *red lighters* because they are always flashing the red stop light at you. Successful entrepreneurs will tell you that whenever they decided to take a big leap of faith, they usually lost a couple of friends along the way. Your real friends are the ones who will encourage your efforts and cheer you on. Many people are jealous cowards and don't like to see someone close to them be brave and move forward. If you want to raise your game, you need to hang out with achievers. It's like playing tennis. If you constantly play with people who are at the same level or who are worse than you, you'll never improve. If you want to raise your game, you need to play with people who are better than you. That's not to say that you need to lose all your friends, but don't hang out too much with the negative ones. Get some new ones who reflect where you want to be. If you want to be successful at something, find someone who's doing it well and copy him or her for a while until you find your way!

John: *I have this great friend Bill, an American guy, who decided to move forward with his life and let go of the people he felt were always holding back. He recorded an outgoing message on his phone that said, "Hi, this is Bill. I* *can't get to the phone right now because I'm busy making a few changes in my life. Leave a message. If I don't get back to you, you're one of those changes."*

Vince: *When people come to our seminars and start our programmes it is because they want to make changes. On more than one occasion we've learnt that someone who has been inspired to go ahead and make those changes has started by leaving a dead-end relationship. These people have realized that the person they've been with for a long time has been holding them back and that they can only move forward without that person. This taking-control-of-your-life game is powerful stuff!*

When you make a decision to change your life you will also rock the worlds of other people, and they may not like it. A person who *wants* change and a person who *doesn't* want change are not really compatible. But everything *is* always changing. Accepting this is what separates the movers-and-shakers from the stuck-in-a-rutters. When we hold on to anything—our beliefs, our money, our possessions—we are acting against nature. Just watch the changing colour of the leaves on the trees every season. *Change is natural.* It's a very odd and fearful mindset that human beings have got into, this thinking they can force things to stay the same.

Why do most people long to win that million playing the lottery? So that they can give up the dead-end jobs that are making them miserable and go on holiday for the rest of their lives. But people who win a million and then do nothing but sit around watching TV and sunbathing on their yachts actually get pretty bored, restless and frustrated in a very short space of time. We are not designed to be mindless, sedentary creatures. We need to do things, to build things, to create things, to be challenged, to think deeply about things … or we will stagnate and wither. The brain is a muscle; it will atrophy if not used.

If you want to change, if you want to learn new skills, if you want to grow exponentially, and build your monetary and moral wealth, be very careful whose company you keep. Obviously you have to keep seeing your family (although if you have a particularly toxic family member you may want to consider putting some distance between you and that person for a certain amount of time while you focus on changing and building your new life) but you *can* choose which friends to spend more time with. Hang out with the ones who are positive, who are also interested in growth. These are the people who will inspire you. You will inspire one another. When meeting new people, consider whether there is positive and productive symbiosis before investing too deeply in a new relationship.

It's natural to seek advice and listen to the opinions of others when you are making big life changes, but beware of unsolicited advice. When people hear of your big plans, of the goals you've set, they will be eager to throw their advice at you and try to guide you. But their advice is based on their opinions and is therefore completely subjective, no matter how trained and qualified they are. Unsolicited mentors can easily throw you off course. It's very easy to get caught up in advice from someone who seems very knowledgeable, especially when you are learning yourself. Pay more attention to someone's *attitude* than attributes. Professional people—for example, lawyers, accountants and doctors—are two a penny. If yours aren't giving you a positive message, go and find ones who are! Just because these people acquired enough knowledge to pass their exams and have developed the skills to practice their professions within accepted guidelines, it does not necessarily make any one of them your best adviser.

One of the most potentially damaging spheres of influence is the media. What you read and hear in the media *must* be taken with a pinch of salt. It is all regurgitated information, brought to you through many filters. Successful entrepreneurs will tell you that the secret to their success was finding a niche in the market: making something that no one had ever thought of, or developing a service that was sorely lacking in people's lives. You are hardly doing that if you start following a trend that is splashed across the front pages of the tabloids.

Consider the old saying "People who know the least know the loudest" and apply that to the media.

Social media can be particularly dangerous, as it is so open to abuse. Every day people get conned by emotional blackmail on social media sites. Every day there are new photos of people in crisis asking for "likes" to support them—requests that go viral. Some of these may be genuine, but the majority are most likely to be dubious organizations gathering data. If you are going to lend your name or profile to an online campaign, don't be surprised if you get hacked or find a bucket load of spam thrown at you!

Even Wikipedia must be treated with a certain amount of caution. Okay, it's well monitored, and any information that is blatantly untrue will be removed, but in many cases the information is still based on the opinions of people who are contributing their thoughts for free and writing their own entries.

So, should you question and challenge what *we* say? Absolutely! Always decide on your own truth and ultimately find your own way.

We're not suggesting you have to do everything differently from everyone else. Obviously we believe we have plenty of good advice to offer. But you should filter all the knowledge you gather through your own judgment system and follow what is right for *you*. Be your own information filter. Gather as much information as you can from as many different sources as you can think of and then decide *for yourself* what you think is true and what you think *your* best course of action is. And then stick with that until you have reason to change it based on further research.

If you came to us tomorrow and said, "Hey, Vince and John, I've got this new idea, you won't believe it. It's contrary to everything you've been teaching, but here's the thing . . . ," we would, of course, listen with open ears.

It's your life; you make your own choices. You are not here to be a carbon copy of your parents, your siblings or your friends. Don't walk in their footsteps; make your own footprints in uncharted territory.

Contrary to what you may have been led to believe, being a successful entrepreneur is not restricted to a minority of people. We live in a meritocracy, a free society: Anyone is free to work hard and build a successful business. If it doesn't work the first time, you make changes and try again. If you are really honest with yourself you might even discover that it's not your negative friends or family members who are stopping you; the only person standing in your way is *you*.

> Our greatest glory is not in never falling, but in rising every time we fall.
>
> —Confucius

What Is Stopping You?

F.E.A.R.: False Evidence Appearing Real!

Our deepest fear is not that we are inadequate.
Our deepest fear is that we are powerful beyond measure.
It is our light, not our darkness, that most frightens us.
We ask ourselves, Who am I to be brilliant, gorgeous, talented, fabulous?
Actually, who are you not to be?

—Marianne Williamson

The biggest roadblock every single one of us faces is our *fear*. Some degree of fear is natural and useful. We *should* be afraid of certain dangers or we will get hurt. But there is a fine line between useful fear and destructive fear.

We've already talked about fear many times, but we cannot stress strongly enough how vital it is to understand your fears and be able to distinguish between rational and irrational fears. The dividing line between the two is a little different for everyone, and most people easily could afford to push the line a little further out and confront some of the fears that they had assumed were rational but actually might be stuff that is holding them back, that could be challenged. Every time you confront and challenge a fear you drastically reduce its impact on you.

Fear is paralyzing. This is important if you are facing a great danger. If you suddenly find yourself at a cliff's edge facing a sheer drop that would undoubtedly kill you, it is important that you freeze. But it is not productive if the fear is not based on something real. If the fear is based on a projection you made of the future, which has not actually happened, or if it is a perceived—rather than actual—danger, then the fear is not conducive to your growth. Many people live their lives in sheer terror even though they're completely unable to verbalize what exactly it is that they're afraid of.

What a great waste of a life.

As Franklin D. Roosevelt said, "We have nothing to fear but fear itself." It is one of those quotes that people hear over and over again without being able to process what it really means (maybe they are *afraid* of accepting what it really means!). It means that our greatest adversary is our *own* fear. If we conquer our fears, we—literally—have nothing to fear!

So what exactly is fear? Where does it come from?

Fear is like a big scary beast standing in your path. What you do with it is your choice. You can stand still and never wrestle with it. Or you can get down and dirty, and fight it. You may lose a few of those battles, but if you keep getting up and trying again, eventually you will wear that beast down and overcome it, which will allow you to move forward and achieve your dreams.

What most people do instead of confronting their fears is bury their heads in the sand. That sand might be their work, or a dysfunctional relationship, or drink, or drugs, or gambling: anything that gives them a buzz, creates a kind of drama, and allows them a means to escape what they can't face looking at.

What are these fears based on? Perhaps a reluctance to grow up and do some hard work. Maybe the so-called root of all evil is immaturity. Many people really don't want to work hard; they don't want to grow up. They want everything handed to them and provided for them, as it was when they were children. There's a general assumption that children born into wealthy families do better than children from poor families. In many cases it is often the other way around, because kids who have everything done for them often don't know the meaning of hard work, while those who have suffered and struggled are often more likely to work as hard as they can to better their lives.

Many people are simply lazy: What they fear is hard work. However, what is even more frustrating than seeing people who are afraid of hard work is watching those who give the *impression* (to themselves as much as anyone else) that they are putting in hours and hours of hard work, when all they are really doing is going around and around in circles, sidestepping anything that feels awkwardly challenging and staying well within their comfort zones. These people are truly tragic because they are deluded; they are conning themselves by putting their inability to move forward down to bad luck or inevitability instead of their own cowardice.

In what is perhaps Shakespeare's greatest soliloquy ("To be or not to be: that is the question …") Hamlet suggests that it is only our fear of the unknown—and more specifically our fear of death—that prevents us from throwing in the towel and opting for suicide when times get tough. Wouldn't we rather

> bear those ills we have
> Than fly to others that we know not of?

And even more poignantly, he concludes

> Thus conscience does make cowards of us all;
> And thus the native hue of resolution
> Is sicklied o'er with the pale cast of thought,
> And enterprises of great pith and moment
> With this regard their currents turn awry,
> And lose the name of action.

Hamlet is saying that the great schemes we resolve to undertake, the plans we make and the declarations we make in the moment, are all futile when we think things over too much, because our fears prevent us from taking action.

Fear is natural. It is part of what makes us human. Our fight-or-flight mechanism is on guard all the time. When we are truly afraid, a chemical reaction takes place and our bodies release adrenalin and noradrenalin into the blood stream. These stress hormones increase our heart rate and blood pressure and make the blood flow away from our extremities towards our heart (which is why people look pale and get cold hands and feet when truly frightened).

Vince: *We need our fight-or-flight response. And we can use it to our advantage. When I go onstage to speak in front of thousands of people I can feel my mouth go dry, my fingers go cold and my heart start pumping faster.*

But these things heighten my awareness and prevent me from making mistakes. They keep me focused on what I have to say and do. Sometimes I think it is less about "feel the fear and do it anyway" (as Susan Jeffers advises) and more about feel the fear and use it to your advantage.

So, rational fear itself is not necessarily a bad thing, and furthermore we can't stop ourselves from feeling it. But we have to learn to harness it, and learn to dispel it when our anxieties are unfounded . . . because 90 percent of our fears *never* materialize. Most of what we imagine never happens. In fact, when things *do* go wrong in life it's usually a scenario you never dreamed of.

That's why we say that most fear is simply **f**alse **e**vidence **a**ppearing **r**eal.

It's the what-if analysis that gives you paralysis.

Far too many people are afraid of what others might think of them. We can suffocate from our obsession with what other people think of us. However, half the time we are actually *projecting* our thoughts onto these people. We attach our own interpretation of their facial expressions to them. We assume we can read their minds.

We should only be afraid of what is rational—what we actually *know*—not what we *assume*. It is a terrible waste of time to base our fears on assumptions. (Remember the old saying: When you *assume*, you make an *ass* out of *u* and *me*!)

But even fears that *are* based on something real and rational can be confronted. These are usually fears about doing something that makes us feel uncomfortable, or the fear of failing and the related fear of the pain that failure will cause. To make the best use of our fears we have to find an optimum state of mind: one in which we are fuelled by the adrenaline of doing something we are afraid of—enough to keep us focused and operating optimally—but in which we are not allowing fear to paralyse us.

What is it that makes people *without* money look at people *with* money and feel resentful? Perhaps they are reminded of their own weaknesses, and need to throw accusations and criticisms out of pure spite and jealousy. But where does that come from? Perhaps it's the fear that they will never be that rich themselves. So perhaps, as Mark Twain suggested, it is a *lack* of money that is the root of all evil. Maybe it is when people are *afraid* of not having enough money or become fearful that they are suddenly going to run out of money one day that they consider doing bad things. So maybe it is not money *or* the lack of money that are the roots of all evil; perhaps it is *fear* that is the root of all evil.

We dearly hope that by showing people how they can always get enough money—how they can create wealth and manage that wealth to ensure that they will always have stability—we can help them eradicate their money worries and therefore eradicate their fears associated with money.

In his book *How to Get Rich* (note: not *How to Get Rich Quick*!), Felix Dennis, the extraordinary millionaire poet, talks about fear as something we have to embrace and then overcome. He explains that successful people are not without fear: They simply conquer it rather than allow it to prevent them from moving forward. He calls fear "the little death, the death by a thousand cuts."

If there is something you are afraid of, something that you don't really want to do but that stands in the way of you reaching your goals, you *must* find a way of working through that fear and doing it. You have to go through the storm to get to the other side. You can't go around the storm. And it's not going to go away.

Vince: *We seem to live in a fear-based society, and that is so unhealthy. I look at my parents and they have lived their whole lives in fear. If something good happens, instead of enjoying it, or celebrating it, they are immediately fearful of it going wrong. That mindset is like a habit they can't break. When I was broke they worried about me all the time. But then when I made some decent money they worried about me losing it. Their attitude is: The further you rise, the further you have to fall. In this respect, they are never happy. They live on an island surrounded by shark-infested waters. They never look at how beautiful the island is because they are constantly looking out at the sharks, feeling afraid. There's a Chinese idiom I love,* 船頭驚鬼, 船尾驚賊, *that basically refers to the fear of being trapped on a boat in which you are always afraid of a ghost that's ahead of you and coming to haunt you, and a thief behind you coming to rob you. You never feel safe aboard this boat of fear.*

Our fears also often come from a place of self-importance . . . from our egos. Embarrassment is a form of fear: We are afraid of what people might think of us. Some people think that they are above doing menial tasks. These people are afraid of taking a job that they deem beneath them. But if that job gets you the money to invest in learning how to better your life, you should never be afraid of doing it.

We each create our own reality, and in the end we only have ourselves to live with and answer to. It does not matter what others think of us; it matters what we think of ourselves. A willingness to be embarrassed, to be humiliated (or what we perceive as humiliation) is an important step along the path to true freedom. Our lives are so short and so small in the grand scheme of things. Why should we care what anyone thinks of us? It's all over in the blink of an eye anyway!

We always challenge people to do what Felix Dennis suggests: to have a **fearless day**—to spend one day of their lives without giving in to fear, to make decisions and take actions that scare the wits out of them, to say yes when they want to say no, to do something they've put off for years because the thought of it terrifies them. When you do this, when you spend a whole day being fearless . . . it can change your life forever. Believe us, there's no going back once you've tasted the buzz of being fearless!

As far as any of us really know for sure, we only have *one life to live.* We believe we all have a duty to make that life count, so do as much with it as you can.

> If you love life, don't waste time, for time is what life is made up of.
>
> —Bruce Lee

The Trap of the Rat Race

Open your eyes, look within. Are you satisfied with the life you're living?

—Bob Marley

What do we mean by the term *rat race*? Presumably the saying comes from the image of rats running around in circles inside glass cabinets in laboratories, going nowhere, with no chance of escaping. But we can also liken the kind of person who is simply hungry for an existence, rather than a life, to a rat.

A race it certainly is: It's a race to get as much money as possible, to accumulate and hoard, always striving to have more than the next rat. The endless pursuit of money for its own sake is not a satisfying pastime by anyone's standards, but we are often taught that it is of utmost importance. Furthermore, we are taught that there is only one way to achieve it: to work hard at school, get our higher education, get a qualification, get a job, keep that job (accepting whatever we can get paid for it), buy a property to live in and raise a family in, and keep working until the day we retire when (fingers crossed) our state and private pensions will be enough for us to live on. We must never step off this path; if we do, we risk failure and destitution.

We are worse than rats: We are *brainwashed* rats!

Countless people get up on Monday morning already looking forward to Saturday; they go back to work in January longing for the next December. They are literally wishing their lives away, caught in a trap where their jobs control them, own their time, and give them a limited salary in exchange for a certain number of hours worked. Many people will tell you they are happy living like this and that the alternative is too risky. Many people say, "This is right for me, I like the security"—but how secure is this existence that's been sold to us as allegedly the right thing? Maybe these people are forcing themselves into a mindset of contentment when deep down they are bored, frustrated and scared of redundancy... which always looms ominously as a real possibility.

When people tell us that they are actually happy in the rat race, we say, great, but don't you still want something to fall back on in case you are ever made redundant? Don't you want added security? With that added security you can still remain in the rat race, but with the knowledge that if at any time you change your mind and decide you *don't* like it you can quit... because you've built some assets and a passive income stream.

What makes us especially frustrated is when people talk positively of their state pensions. They are giving money, every year, to a bunch of money managers (who always pay themselves a fee before investing the money) to throw around in the stock market. Most people have no idea how little their state pensions will give them when they retire. The amount will barely feed them, let alone provide them with any comfort.

Vince: *My friend worked in IT for years. He was very successful; he had worked his way up to where he commanded a really decent salary. He always told me he was perfectly happy doing what he did and that he didn't consider himself to be part of the rat race because it was his choice to work as hard as he did. Then one day out of the blue he got made redundant because the company he worked for was taken over. It was a complete shock and a terrible blow to him as he had a family to support. After years of rejecting my invitations he recently attended one of our seminars.*

John: *I have an aunt who used to be a buyer for a big sportswear chain. She loved her job; she loved her life. She got to travel all around the world. She had kids and a very supportive husband, but she was the breadwinner... until she got made redundant. After years of being completely uninterested (bordering on the critical) in what I do she has recently done an about-turn. She called and asked me for some advice. She sounded very subdued as she told me what had happened. She said she wanted to start talking to me about what I do; she was ready to take more control over her financial future.*

We're not saying that everyone should become full-time entrepreneurs, but we do believe that everyone has the right to learn entrepreneurial skills so that they have the ability to take control of their financial futures. Yes, we need people doing menial jobs, or the country would grind to a halt, but those people in menial jobs should still have the opportunity to learn what their options are. We believe we have a responsibility to show *everyone* that they *do* have choices, that they don't have to accept verbatim what they've been taught by their educational system and the people they perceive to be their superiors.

We are taught that it is safe to put our money in banks and that the banks will always look after our savings. The people of Cyprus (where the government raided individual savings accounts to bail itself out in 2013) will tell you a different story!

There are so many important life skills that are not taught at school. We are not taught about managing our money and investing for the future; we are taught how to work out the hypotenuse of a right-angled triangle. For what purpose? We are not taught how to operate a washing machine or raise children. Perhaps we're expected to learn these skills from our parents—but they're out working full-time in the rat race in order to put food on the table. They're completely exhausted most days, and no one taught them parenting skills either, so we're all in the dark.

We all have different reasons for getting stuck in the rat race. Mostly what keeps us there is fear of the unknown, as well as not believing that we have the time, energy or money to change things. It's a vicious circle.

If you don't leave school at 16 (like Richard Branson), you'll probably follow a traditional path. Maybe you'll do well at school and go on to university. Then you'll hopefully get a good degree and leave with debts of around £30,000. So then you'll have to get a job to start paying off that debt. Of course you'll need somewhere to live, so you need to get a job that pays you enough to cover your repayments on your debt, your rent, and your car payments (because you'll probably have to borrow more money to get a car to take you to your job). After a while, hopefully your salary will increase, but by then you'll want to buy a house—so you'll get into more debt by taking out a mortgage, which means that there will be no way you can ever leave your job because you are committed to a mortgage and a car loan, and you're still paying off your student loans. Then you'll live in fear of being made redundant because you have so many debt repayments that depend on your salary.

It's not so much the rat race, anymore: It's the *trap* race!

The Truth about Your Job

We've been told:

Work hard and you'll keep getting promoted.

The undesirable truth is:

As soon as you can, you should work for yourself.

When you work for someone else, it doesn't matter how much effort you put in, you will only ever get a limited return on your time investment. You can put in 100 percent, but you'll only ever get a percentage (say, around 50 percent) back. Okay, you are guaranteed that 50 percent, but it won't ever change. When you work for yourself and you put in 100 percent, you have every chance of getting 100 percent back. Okay, sometimes you might get much less back than that, for a while you could even get 0 percent (because it always takes time to get financial results), but in the end you are always potentially looking at a full return on your investment!

There are worker bees and there are queen bees, and we need both in order for a capitalist society to work. But so many people stay miserable as worker bees because they don't understand that they have the potential to be queen bees. Sure, not everyone *wants* to be a queen bee, but everyone should be shown how to become one in case they want to give it a go. Young people in particular are often kept in their places by jealous business owners who are threatened by their talents. When mean-spirited business owners find particularly talented workers, they don't want those workers going off and starting rival businesses, so it is in the interest of the business owners not to encourage those workers too much. Never let someone else tell you what you are worth.

Consider the following case studies of people trapped in the rat race. Perhaps you know someone like one of these people—or perhaps you'll even recognize elements of your *own* life in some of these examples.

Judith grew up in Cardiff. She was the youngest of three girls. She found school a real challenge, academically. She was great at art but couldn't concentrate on anything else. She got frustrated and misbehaved, so she was labelled a troublemaker and was often told she was stupid. She grew up believing she was stupid. She always lacked confidence, and had to work extra hard to make friends and hold down jobs. Eventually, she joined an animation company in a low-level job and worked her way up, but she feels trapped by the cutthroat culture and the competition to see who stays in the office longest. At 32, she lives in permanent fear of being sacked and not being able to get another job.

Mark worked hard at school. He did well and went on to a good university to study engineering. He was always popular. Nothing bad ever happened to him. He came from a good, stable home. Eventually he met a girl, married her, and started a family of his own. He got a great job working for an engineering firm and quickly rose through the ranks. But as his salary increased so did the number of hours he was expected to work. He and his wife started arguing about how little time he spent with the family. Then he got a promotion and worked even longer hours. To compensate he encouraged his wife to buy a bigger house and to live lavishly. One day he got made redundant after the company lost a big contract. He couldn't get another job and sank into a deep depression. His outgoings were huge and eventually the house was under threat of repossession. He and his wife managed to sell it just in time, but their marriage was over. The house sale was followed by a divorce and his relationship with his children suffered greatly as a result. At 50, he doesn't know what he has to look forward to.

Kevin grew up in a troubled home. He father was a violent alcoholic who beat him regularly and his mother suffered from clinical depression. Kevin moved into a small room in a men's hostel when he was 18, after failing to get any A levels at school. He started working in a supermarket, earning just enough to cover his rent and buy food. He borrows money from friends, and his only enjoyment is smoking and going to the pub. He lives for his weekends. He has no passion for life and has never had a long-term girlfriend. However, a girl he had a one-night stand with has become pregnant. He is about to become a father for the first time and is terrified. He wants to contribute to support the child, but he has no idea where to begin to find the extra money. At 25, he feels trapped and terrified; he has been drinking more than usual to escape the fear.

Rachel works for a top investment bank in the city. She makes £250,000 per year in base salary, plus bonuses. She often works 16-hour days. She uses cocaine to boost her confidence and regularly drinks more than a bottle of red wine a night. The drugs and alcohol are part of the culture of the banking world; there are big lunches and even bigger parties to attend with clients. She has no time for a relationship even though she is desperately lonely. She is always trying to keep up with the city boys. She's terrified that she's not going to be able to close a deal she's been working on for months. She knows she'll lose her job if she fails. She can't take the pressure anymore. To avoid hitting rock bottom, she takes two weeks off and checks into a rehab clinic for drug and alcohol dependency. She has no idea how this is going to affect her career; she's too tired to think about it. She's 34 and exhausted.

These people deserve a break! They deserve to be shown that there are other options available, rather than the dead-end lives they feel they are currently living.

John: *I remember so clearly being part of the rat race and it makes my blood run cold when I think about it. I remember dragging myself up in the morning, racing for the train, having to stand because it was so packed, getting off at the other end, going down endless escalators into the Tube, and spending another 15 minutes squished between a woman reeking of perfume and a man who'd clearly drunk the contents of a brewery the night before but hadn't been home and was staggering into work in yesterday's crumpled shirt. The mingled aromas of Chanel No. 5 and stale beer do not make a pleasant environment at 8:45 A.M. And it was like the movie* Groundhog Day*; I was doing exactly the same thing day in and day out. I never knew what day of the week it was during that commute. I felt like a zombie and thought, this isn't life; this is torture.*

Vince: *We don't tell people to give up their day jobs before they know how they are going to replicate the income they've been earning—obviously it is vital to have a source of income—but we do teach them how to plan for freedom. We feel that planning for freedom is a better goal than planning to be trapped in the rat race indefinitely.*

CHAPTER 10

It's about Work, Stupid!

Being good in business is the most fascinating kind of art. Making money is art and working is art and good business is the best art.

—Andy Warhol

In his successful 1992 U.S. presidential campaign, Bill Clinton used the phrase "It's the economy, stupid" to express what voters were most concerned about (the sluggish recovery from the recession that occurred during George H. W. Bush's four-year term). The phrase has since been adapted to express all statements of the obvious. And it is stating the obvious to say that the only thing that can make you wealthy is ... *work*! However, people love to be sold on the idea that there is some secret, some scheme that can get them rich without having to work. Well, there is one ... it's called the lottery, and you have a 14-million-to-1 chance of winning it. Go ahead!

We're not serious, of course. We've already criticized the lottery for preying on people's fears and laziness: It's just gambling, with terrible odds. The other way in which we feel people get conned into thinking that they can get rich without working is the message put about by many of those positive-thinking or law of attraction self-help books that seem to suggest people can make a wish and then sit around waiting for it to come true. As we've said before, there *is* value in positive thinking—it just needs to be coupled with positive *working*.

But there's yet another way in which people are sold the idea that riches can be gained without working hard: through the media machine that paints lavish pictures of celebrity lifestyles without telling the whole story.

In an interview with Ellen DeGeneres, after he'd spoken at the Teen Choice Awards in 2013, Ashton Kutcher spoke out against the "propaganda machine" that promotes fame and celebrity as lifestyle choices. In the speech he gave at the awards ceremony, Kutcher talked about the importance of hard work and taking advantage of every opportunity you see. He'd also said that "being sexy" had nothing to do with what the media sells it as, and that instead it is about being "smart, thoughtful, and generous." And then he noted how he was reminded, by working on a movie about Steve Jobs, of the fact that life is simply what we make of it. He urged his young fans to remember that, as Jobs famously said, "everything around us, that we call life, was made up by people who are no smarter than you, and you can build your own things, you can build your own life that other people can live in. So build a life. Don't live one, build one." He is a huge advocate of teaching young children to build something, to achieve real results in life and to invest their money wisely in order to see it grow. Kutcher himself is a big investor in start-up businesses and the stock market.

We're constantly being sold a totally false reality by the media. If you believed everything you read, you'd think that rich and famous people never did a hard day's work in their lives. The media also makes it seem as if the rich don't have to go through any of the pain average people go through, as if they are somehow set apart from us. We watch celebrities get pregnant and seemingly have miraculously painless births, walking out of hospital a few days later having not gained a pound. Maybe the rumours that they book in for a Caesarean and tummy tuck on the same day are true! Some celebrities, apparently, are too posh to push! Most real women will tell you that you can't have the baby without the pain.

Celebrity lifestyles might be portrayed in the media as being luxurious and idyllic, but the sad fact is many celebrities struggle with the loss of privacy and freedom. Some even get deeply depressed about it and turn to drink and drugs to escape.

Vince: *Leslie Cheung was a famous pop and movie star in Hong Kong in the 1980s. He was a real hero of mine, so I remember being distraught when he committed suicide by jumping off the Mandarin Oriental hotel in Hong Kong. He was only 46—the age I am at the time of writing! He had reportedly talked* *to relatives, who knew he was suffering from depression, during the year before he took his own life. He apparently kept questioning why he felt so down and so bad when he had everything a person might want—money, success, fame, good looks, and so on. He was baffled as to why he felt as depressed as he did. He wrote in his suicide note, "Why does it have to be like this?"*

Why do you think so many celebrities get hooked on drugs, some even tragically taking their own lives as a result? Because what they thought it would be like to be famous, and what it is *actually* like being famous, is chalk and cheese. But the media can't expose this because if people knew, *X Factor* couldn't exist. Why do hundreds of thousands of hopefuls line up for a chance to get on that show year after year? A small handful of them are genuinely looking for an opportunity to get that elusive recording contract so that they can get paid to do the work they love, but the majority are there because they are hungry for fame. Once they fail to get onto *X Factor* they probably start applying for *Big Brother.* If only they knew . . . having photographers camped outside their houses every minute of the day, or having an old flame selling embarrassing kiss-and-tell stories to the tabloids and discovering that the only way to make money is to sell their own sides of those sordid stories to the same tabloid because no employer wants to hire them, is not the fabulous lifestyle they envisaged when they were filling out their online applications to get on TV. These people want to dodge hard work by getting famous. But dealing with fame is a harder job than the average person can cope with.

Vince: *I once knew an artist who was always broke. She claimed she couldn't get a real job because then she would have no time to do her art. But she wasn't making any money from her art so she was always borrowing money and claiming government benefits. This depressed her so she wasn't inspired to create any art. It looked like a pretty futile vicious circle to me. If she'd put some effort into building a passive income by putting a few years' hard work into building a business to provide her with an income to take care of her basic needs she could have had all the time in the world to work on her art. And she would have been able to invest in some nice new materials to boot!*

Most people are put off by working harder because someone else owns their time, but when you are investing in your own business it pays to work harder and smarter.

The Truth about Work

We've been told:

You can only make more money by working longer hours.

The undesirable truth is:

You need to work smarter by doing more in the time you have and increasing your hourly rate for the time you spend working.

When you work for someone, that person pays you for your time. You are given a salary based on the hours you work. Everyone has an hourly rate they work for. Say you are on a salary of £35,000 per year. Divide that by 261 days (365 less 104 weekend days) and you get £134 per day. If you work for 8 hours in the day, that's an hourly rate of around £16–17, and that's pre-tax. In the end, you'll only get around £12 per hour. And you thought £35,000 was a good salary! Compare that with running a company that's generating an annual profit of £10 million. Your hourly rate in this scenario would be £4,789. And you'll only be taxed on what you don't spend on business expenses. When you are an employee the tax is taken out of your salary at the source, and you can't deduct any business expenses. Owning a business and working for yourself will always be a better way of earning money than being an employee.

John: *When I realized my life was slipping through my fingers while I worked long hours for someone else's profits I decided to dedicate myself to working smarter. I wanted to maximize my hourly rate so that I could make as much as possible for the time I put in. To begin with, I worked every waking hour, much longer hours than I'd worked at my salaried job. But it paid off because as my business grew, my hourly rate skyrocketed, and my downtime increased. Now I make sure I am maximizing my opportunities in every hour I work. I know property developers who will go into a property to fix a toilet because they perceive it as saving money on a handyman. But if I'm doing that for an hour, I'm losing time in which I could be making a deal or researching a property lead. I took a massive risk to get where I am today. It wasn't easy to part with the £10,000 that I invested in getting my first deal, but it bought me the education I needed to become a property investor. It was terrifying. But it paid off.*

You can't buy more time, but you can maximize the value of your time, both in terms of what you make during the time you're working and in terms of the quality of what you do with your downtime.

So, . . . if you're ready to start working—probably harder than you've ever worked in your life—we're ready to tell you what you need to do!

> Don't go around saying the world owes you a living. The world owes you nothing. It was here first.
>
> —Mark Twain

PART III

THE HOW

In this section, we are going to help you design your blueprint for building infinite wealth. You must have a clear plan, first and foremost. If you want something, but you haven't made a plan, there is little chance you're going to get it. Every single successful businessperson in the world has a plan. You must make a plan that clearly sets out, step-by-step, what you are going to do and when you are going to do it. Your plan is your strategy; it is the list of the actions you have committed to take in order to make massive changes in your life.

CHAPTER 11

The Wealth Superhighway

If you don't design your own life plan, chances are you'll fall into someone else's plan. And guess what they have planned for you? Not much.

—Jim Rohn

What is your current **wealth strategy**? What's your plan? How are you intending to take care of yourself and your family when you retire? Are you relying on your state pension? If so, do you know exactly how little that is going to give you every month? Have you taken out a private pension? If so, did it survive the last financial crash? The financial world got upended in the last crisis. Have you made any plans to protect yourself if that happens again? Do you know how to make as much (if not more) money in a recession as you can make during a time of economic growth? Do you understand how derivatives work and how they can work for you? Do you trade the financial markets? Are you investing in property? Do you have a business?

If you're a little overwhelmed by our questions and your answer to the "what's your plan" question is "I buy lottery tickets every week and I always use the same numbers, so I'm really banking on a win at some point" (we kid you not, people actually say this), then there is something seriously wrong. Only you can decide upon the details, but you *must* have a plan as to how you are going to support yourself when you stop working.

The Truth about Your Pension

We've been told:

Pay into your company or private pension scheme to supplement your state pension when you retire.

The undesirable truth is:

Build your own pension fund that you *control.*

When you put money into a big pension fund you are basically giving your hard-earned pennies to someone else to gamble with. With the stock market so unstable and unregulated, no one can guarantee you are going to get the pension you expect when you retire. Even your state pension that you have been forced to contribute to through your National Insurance deductions is not going to give you anything close to a basic standard of living. More and more people are finding out that they cannot afford to retire when they thought they were going to be able to. If you want to guarantee that you're able to retire at a certain age, and if you want to have money with which to enjoy your retirement, you need to learn how to manage and invest your money so that you're guaranteed a decent income stream.

The ideal plan for a truly secure future has three distinct levels: investing in appreciable assets, creating passive income, and building a valuable business brand. Not everyone will get to that final stage of building a business because not everyone believes they have a valuable business idea (a belief we are going to challenge later on), but everyone needs a plan that will at least give them money to live on if and when they can no longer work (whether through an inability to work or a *desire* not to work!).

Imagine a motorway with three lanes and the hard shoulder, as shown in Figure 11.1. In the hard shoulder you are stationary; you are not even moving forward. This is where you are if you are simply relying on your monthly salary to make ends meet and assuming your state pension will look after you in old age. In this scenario there are no savings, nothing for the future, nothing coming in passively: in other words, no real wealth.

Now imagine you move into the slow lane. You start to move at a reasonable pace. This represents when you have started to invest in appreciable assets, most likely property. Now your wealth is growing, slowly. You have some momentum in your wealth creation.

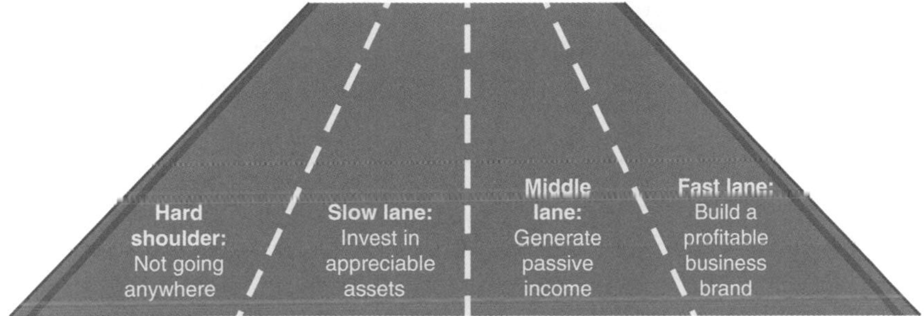

Figure 11.1 The Motorway of Wealth and Success

At a certain point, all being well, you should be able to move into the middle lane. This is where you start creating ongoing passive income. This is most likely your rental income but it could also be supplemented by income from other investments and activities, for example, trading the Forex market.

Finally, in the fast lane, you start creating a business and building a brand. If you can build a successful business, become a known expert in your field, and position yourself ahead of your competition, your wealth will grow exponentially.

Asset Building

You *must* have appreciable assets in order to have infinite wealth.

The most accessible way for most people to acquire appreciable assets is to invest in property. If you are an antiques expert or an art dealer, by all means focus on those appreciable assets; however, most of those specialist industries require expert knowledge that takes years to acquire. You need expert knowledge in order to invest in property, too, but this knowledge is easier and quicker to learn. And in any case, property is everyone's concern: We all have to live somewhere. Whether we own or rent we all pay to live somewhere, so it pays to know as much as you can about the industry. Plus, there is no shortage of property; it's a massive market so there's room for everyone. Monetary wealth is dependent on owning appreciable assets. When you have equity in a property, that is an appreciable asset. It may fluctuate a little with the housing market, but in the long term property goes up in value and you don't use it up on a daily basis as you use up cash.

Here's the question we are most often asked: *How do I invest in property if I have no money?*

Obviously it is easier to start investing in property if you have money, but if you don't, it is by no means impossible. If you don't have any money the chances are that you have *time*. If you think you don't have time you need to *make* some, or you will never get out of the rat race!

If you are time-rich and cash-poor, you need to team up with someone who is cash-rich and time-poor. Remember, smart investors will always get people working for them. Entrepreneurs are traditionally very savvy at maximizing their resources, and that means going into business with people who have what they need. What most busy, successful entrepreneurs need more of is time, and if you have time you can offer them something of value in exchange for the money to invest in property.

When you approach someone you'd like to partner with, you must know exactly what you are offering. If you ask for a cash investment from someone you must be clear on the projected return on investment and the payback period. An investor also needs to know what kind of security you can offer and, of course, what the value proposition is. You need to be able to tell the investor the exact details of what you offer and why it would be a good idea to invest in you. You need to show your passion and hunger for an idea. Investors want to see evidence of your commitment. They need to see that you are overflowing with energy and enthusiasm for your chosen venture.

Don't forget that intangible assets can be appreciable, too. We mostly associate intangible assets with business creation. A business in itself is—potentially—an appreciable asset, made up of assets that are tangible (your goods and equipment) and assets that are intangible (your brand, reputation, and knowledge). Intangible assets are all part of your business's value. Some intangible assets can actually be measured on a business's balance sheet—a company's brand, any patents it holds, and its goodwill (the amount another company would pay to acquire the business in excess of its actual net value) can all have value.

But your greatest intangible asset is . . . *you*!

You are actually your most valuable asset.

While you live and breathe you have unlimited potential value and an opportunity to become wealthy. And no one has more control over *how* wealthy you can become than you. You are your own best asset. If your house burnt down, your business went bust, the insurance didn't pay out, and you were left bankrupt, you would *still* have your own skills and experience. It's so easy for people to forget this after a big catastrophe. You could be homeless, couch surfing, or living on the streets, but you *still* have value because no one can destroy *your* skills, *your* experience, *your* creativity and *your* knowledge. Never forget that.

And this is why you should invest in your greatest asset (*you*) wisely.

How much do you value yourself? Are you investing in your well-being? Are you educating yourself? Do you make sure you get enough sleep and healthy food? Do you do a healthy amount of exercise (neither overdoing it nor doing too little)? Do you have healthy relationships? Do you protect yourself from toxic people? Do you *enjoy* life?

If you are not taking the greatest care of your most valuable asset, you can have all the money you want in the bank, but your worth will never reach its full potential.

So step one of your plan is **invest in appreciable assets, starting with the first and most important one . . . *you*!**

Passive Income Generation

The most obvious source of passive income when you are building a property portfolio is your rental income. That is half the purpose (after the capital gains from appreciation) of owning investment property.

But there are more ways to create passive income. You could start a business. If you are not ready for that step yet, you could look at trading the money markets.

In *Goals to Gold: Trading the Football Pitch for the Financial Markets*, ex-footballer Lee Sandford shows us how he created a healthy passive income when his football career ended by learning to trade the financial markets. We love to criticize the huge salaries of footballers, but we forget that their careers are fleeting. They retire before most people have sent all of their kids though primary school. It is imperative that they invest their money wisely and work out a good financial plan to support them in the future. Sadly, many of them don't do this and end up in trouble—sometimes even bankrupt.

As Sandford points out in his book, the Forex (foreign currency exchange) market is by far the most straightforward market to trade in. Most people have a good grasp on exchanging one currency for another, and, unlike stocks and shares, there's little chance of losing all your money (because it's highly unlikely that a major currency would be devalued to zero against another major country's currency—the last time that happened was before World War II when the German mark was devalued to a level where it was almost worthless) so the risk is limited.

Financial wizards and economists all have their opinions on investing, along with various strategies, but we feel that trading the Forex market is best for newcomers to trading because it is the easiest to grasp.

However, trading is a skill that requires some investment in terms of education. Invest some time learning how to do it before you give it a go.

Trading the Forex market, like any kind of investing, still carries a certain amount of risk, and it would be unwise to go ahead and start trading without learning the ropes first, but once you feel you know what you are doing you should go for it. Too many people steer clear of any risk at all and stagnate as a result. We have to take a certain amount of risk if we want to move forward.

The Truth about Risk

We've been told:

Don't take too many risks.

The undesirable truth is:

Take calculated risks whenever and wherever you can, because there is no progress without risk.

Think where the world and the human race would be today if no explorer had ever risked going into the unknown. So many lands would have remained uncharted, so many cultures would have stayed unknown and so many ocean depths would have been unexplored. Even today people take great risks to show us the wonders of the natural world. Documentary filmmakers sit in boats in shark-infested seas or lie amongst ravenous lions in order to bring us never-before-seen footage. It's the same in business. People risk their money investing in technology, spending huge sums on research and development, and going through successes and failures, so that we can enjoy new innovations such as smartphones and (coming sooner than you think) self-driving cars. In *Without Risk There's No Reward*, Bob Mayer tells many anecdotes to show how his booming property business could not have been built without taking huge risks.

Step two of your plan should be to **create a passive income from rental income and through trading the money markets, with a possible long-term view to creating a passive income from a business**.

Business Creation and Brand Building

Does building a business sound like hard work? It is. But it is a highly effective way of creating passive income, as well as building a potentially appreciable asset. Remember that assets can be tangible or intangible. A brand is an intangible asset. Coca-Cola's huge worth is based on its brand, not the actual value of the contents of its products. Knowledge is an intangible asset. People often forget that investing in their own skills and knowledge is a good investment.

What stops many people from starting a business is not knowing what business to start. Obviously it is critical to get the decision right. If you choose a business that you are not passionate about you will not work hard enough at it. If you choose a business that is not specialized enough, that does not stand out in an overcrowded market, you will be swallowed up by the competition.

You should only choose to build a business that you feel passionately about. Remember that when you love what you do enough, it never feels like work. As John's mum always told him, if you find something that you love doing and that you can make a living from you'll never work another day in your life.

When we ask people what it is that they do that is special, that they are best at, that makes them stand out, they often struggle to answer. Why? Because most of us are raised to believe that we must fit in.

Why do we work so hard to fit in when we were born to stand out?

Everyone has the potential to be an expert at something. If you know more than the average Joe about a topic, you are an expert in it. We all have unique skills if we take the time to identify them. What are the issues that people come to you for advice on? What is it that everyone is always asking *you* about? What do your friends and family always say you are so good at doing?

Whatever that is, it is probably something that you have, or can do, that adds value to people's life. Chances are you've been giving it away for free. How do you make unlimited money from it? You offer it for a fee. Then, if you can, you offer it to multiple people at the same time—a group of people who each pay you a fee. Then (if possible and ideally) you teach others how to offer it to even more people and charge them a licensing fee that they pay to you for permission to use or do it. And bingo! You have franchised yourself.

This strategy is so old and so powerful that many people have used—and even abused—it. In the United States in the 1990s there was a particularly aggressive spate of multilevel marketing schemes that sold people on the profits that could be made from a business franchise without properly educating them on how to run that business. Many companies came under fire for selling expensive franchises (in terms of investment in product inventory and training seminars) in schemes that were really nothing more than a way for the people higher up in the chain to offload a huge amount of inventory and make large commissions on educational material.

This is very different from finding *your own* niche business and teaching others your unique skills.

In order to maximize your business potential, you need to narrow your niche down as much as you can. Find that one specific thing that *you* are best at.

First figure out your niche, then look for a *micro* niche under that, and finally try to work out your *nano* niche.

Here's a great example. Say you are a makeup artist with exceptional skills at making eye makeup look good. Your niche would be personal grooming, your micro niche would be makeup, and your nano niche would be eye makeup.

Here's another example. You are a wedding planner who has a great reputation for planning unforgettable weddings in romantic European cities (you know how to get around language barriers, have the best deals on group bookings in hotels, know the best local chefs, and so on). Your niche would be wedding planning, your micro niche would be destination weddings, and your nano niche would be planning weddings in European cities (as opposed to, say, destination beach weddings).

If you can find a highly desirable nano niche that no one else has tapped into and it's clear that people would pay for that product or service, you are set to make a huge amount of money!

Ultimately, it's all about positioning.

We've seen a personal trainer reposition himself as a body transformation expert. He's gone from earning £50 a session to earning £3,000 a session and now only works with major celebrities. If you're a wedding planner you'll want to be *the* bespoke wedding designer: the person people will automatically approach when they want to create unforgettable weddings. If you are going to create personal computers you'll want to create the ones that everyone will want; that is, ones that are unique and beautiful with classic style that need no instruction manual because you can just take them out of the box and start using them. Computers that are so sexy and exciting that even if you have one you want the next version just because you love it so much. Computers that make you feel like you belong to the coolest computer club in the world. (Well, you can't do that because Apple did it already, but you get the point!)

A huge part of a successful business is how you present yourself. You can't hide behind nerves or shyness. You have to have the confidence to get up on a stage in front of thousands of people to talk about and sell your business. If you struggle with the idea of doing that, then you need to get help with building your confidence. Every successful businessperson has to be good at public speaking. If it doesn't come naturally, they learn how to get good at it. If you're not confident, *learn* how to be more confident. You must be able to work with people if you want to build a successful business. Multimillionaire entrepreneurs are not shy. If they once were, they learnt how to get over their shyness.

Your business is *you*. Present yourself in the best possible light. Remember, you need to stand out!

Never before has there been such a total meritocratic environment for entrepreneurs. Anyone can launch a website. It's relatively cheap. We can trade on a global scale thanks to credit cards and payment systems such as PayPal. We can market to anyone through the Internet.

But a meritocracy is a double-edged sword: It removes barriers to entry whilst increasing competition. And that's why you need to do everything you can to stand out.

These days it is not so much about who you know as **who knows you**!

And before anyone knows you, you must *know yourself* and know what you are selling. Know exactly what skills you are selling, what your strengths and weaknesses are, how you come across in a business meeting, and what value your business adds to the lives of your clients and customers. If you have gaps in your knowledge and skills, plug them by creating partnerships with others. No one ever built a successful business alone! The most successful businesspeople are very clear on which skills they possess and which ones they need to acquire by hiring staff. Find people who have what you need and need what you have.

There's an old saying we love that goes, "If you're the smartest person in your business, you're going to be broke." You need to hire people who are smarter than you. When you put together many people with different skill sets you will find that the whole is greater than the sum of the parts. That's great *business synergy*.

Step three of your plan hopefully will be to **build a successful business.**

The Path to Infinite Wealth

After the "How do you invest in property if you have no money?" question, the next one we most often get asked is "What do you mean by *infinite wealth*?"

Before we answer that question, let's look at the stages of the journey that lead to infinite wealth.

Now that we know wealth comes from building appreciable assets, creating passive income, and then growing a strongly branded business, we can look at the four stages of the path towards infinite wealth. They are:

1. Financial security
2. Financial freedom
3. Financially rich
4. Financially abundant

Financial Security

On 6 January 2014, Chancellor George Osbourne gave a speech at Warwickshire-based car part manufacturing company Sertec to mark its announcement that it was creating 400 new jobs. The speech was widely covered by the British media because it came at a time that the British economy was believed to be making a marked recovery. At one point during his speech Osbourne said, "You all know there's no better financial security than having a job." *Wrong!* There is no better financial security than owning appreciable assets. A job is simply a monthly pay cheque. What happens when that pay cheque suddenly stops coming in because you've been made redundant?

People believe they are secure when they have money in the bank and a job to go to. But both of those could cease to exist at the drop of a hat. Most people, if they were made redundant without pay (all too possible during difficult economic times due to companies going bankrupt), could only last a couple of months without a salary. Your **financial security** is basically what you have stored away for living expenses if money stopped coming in. Most people have around £6,000 saved somewhere. The average person spends approximately £2,000 a month on their living costs. That means that the average person could live for only three months before the money runs out. After that point it's a slippery slope. When you stop paying mortgage repayments the bank is going to repossess your house, and then you have to find somewhere to live, making it harder to get a new job. Many people saw their entire worlds collapse like this during the most recent recession. What we have been *led* to believe is financial security is really false security. So it doesn't make sense to budget for that kind of financial security; if you want real security you have to budget for financial freedom.

Financial Freedom

You can't get financially **rich** (the third stage of the path towards infinite wealth) until you are financially **free**. So how do you achieve financial freedom? You are financially free when you have a passive income that covers your living costs. This buys you back your time so that you can spend it investing in getting financially rich. If you need £2,000 a month to live on then you need to invest in something that will provide you with £2,000 *without you having to get out of bed*. Of course you *are* going to get out of bed, but you are going to get out of bed to spend your time building the business that is going to make you rich—so the £2,000 needs to come in as a passive income. Remember, being self-employed is not the same as having a business. When you are self-employed you are still working for people in order to make the money you need to live on; you are still living on your *active* income. The aim is to have a source of income, such as rental income, that comes to you without you actively working on a daily basis for it; a source that makes money *passively* for you. Once you have an automated business (such as a property portfolio providing rental income) that makes your monthly nut (what you need to live on), no matter where in the world you are or what you are doing, you have achieved financial freedom. And now your time is free so that you can become financially rich.

Financially Rich

When you are financially rich you have enough wealth to enable you to live comfortably for the rest of your life and even leave a legacy when you die. You could liquidate your assets and never need to work again because your assets far outweigh your liabilities. Bill Gates is rich because he has so many assets. One of his assets just happens to be a company called Microsoft, which, according to a January 2014 report in *Forbes*, has a market capitalization value of $200 billion! The term *high net worth* has been creeping into the popular vernacular in recent years. People seem more inclined to refer to themselves as being high net-worth people, or high net-worth families, rather than as rich people or rich families. This is related to the fact (as we described at the beginning of this book) that wealth has less to do with money in the bank and more to do with a favourable balance of assets against liabilities. And you don't always need to use cash to increase your net worth. Companies regularly use stock instead of cash in their mergers and acquisitions. Of course, once you are financially rich you could argue that there is no turning back. You are now open to become financially abundant.

Financially Abundant

Being financially abundant is not really about your net worth or the number of assets you own, or how much money you have in the bank: It's about your mindset. Being financially abundant is having the attitude that you can afford to give it all away because you know it will all come back to you. (Perhaps—going back to an earlier point we made—partly because you know that the core wealth you own is *you.*) It sounds a bit strange at first, but financial abundance really is an actual state of mind. Why are some of the wealthiest people in the world also the most generous, the most philanthropic (most people who are worth billions give a huge amount away every year)? They don't hoard their wealth and they are not afraid to give because they know having wealth entails an ongoing fluctuation of money coming in and money going out. They never look at their money as being static; it's always moving. We've all heard of bankers earning their

£1 million bonuses and blowing that money on fast cars and yachts. Are they abundantly wealthy? They are not even close. Warren Buffett reportedly draws down an annual salary of $100,000 and gives a percentage of his profits to charity every year. Maybe it's because he knows that he could never actually give it *all* away—it would keep coming back to him. Why is that? Is it karma? Is it partly the law of attraction? Who knows? But it works.

John: *I know having an abundant mindset works because I've experienced it. I'll never forget the moment I started to be aware of it. I was in a petrol station filling up. I paid for my petrol and there was a charity box on the counter. I reached into my pocket for some change and pulled out a £50 note. I smiled and thought, why not? I put it in the box and drove home. Only an hour after that happened, a new deal came through. It was worth a fortune. From that moment on, things like this kept happening to me. I'd make some really generous gesture, such as giving a lot of money to some person who needed it or leaving a huge tip, and almost immediately a big deal would come in. I'm not that superstitious—I'm quite a down-to-earth guy—but I can't deny what I keep experiencing.*

Vince: *It's hard to grasp the concept of abundance, but take a moment to look out of the window. If it's daytime, look at the branches on a tree, or the leaves, or the blades of grass on the ground or the grains of sand on a beach. If it's night, look at the stars in the sky. Just find something outside, in nature, that there seems to be an infinite number of. These sorts of things just go on and on endlessly: You could never count them all. You know there are more stars than you can actually see out of your window, more sand, more trees and leaves. Think of money like that. There is an infinite amount of it around. No one is stopping you from getting it; we all have access to it, and, unlike the infinite celestial objects you can see in the night sky, you don't have to build a space rocket to get to it!*

Financial abundance sounds nice, doesn't it? It's probably a long way off from where you are now, and you have to go through each of the four stages of the path towards infinite wealth to get there (you can't skip any steps), but you can practice the mindset in preparation!

The psychologist Abraham Maslow suggested in the 1940s that we have a hierarchy of needs, which we illustrate in a pyramid form in Figure 11.2. His theory stressed that we can't skip a level of the pyramid: If we don't have our basic needs met, we can't get our higher needs met. The same goes for building monetary wealth through

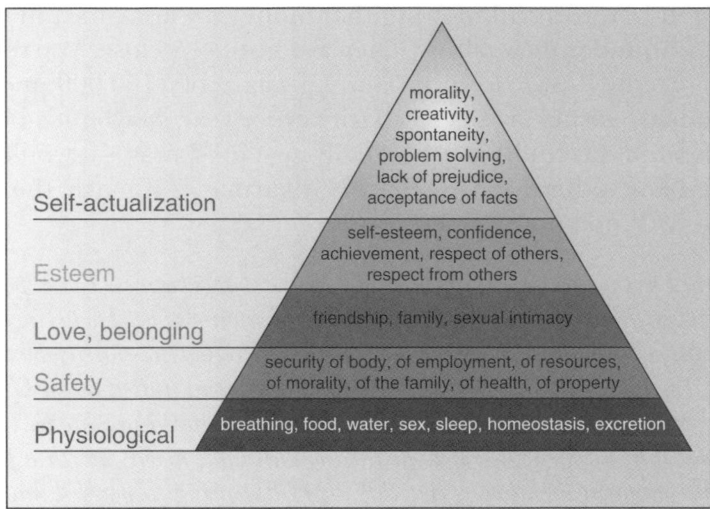

Figure 11.2 Maslow's Hierarchy of Needs
Source: Wikipedia, 2007.

the four stages. You simply can't reach financial abundance without going through and achieving the previous stages. You have to stack up the building blocks in order to reach the top of the pyramid.

So now we are ready to share with you exactly what we mean when we talk of *infinite wealth.* It's not an actual figure on a balance sheet or a static measure of net worth: It's a state of mind . . . it's the acceptance of *financial abundance,* which is the knowledge that there is no limit to how much wealth you can acquire, because you know you can keep on finding it and creating it.

CHAPTER 12

The More Money Mindset

The possession of anything begins in the mind.

—Bruce Lee

We know we've made the concepts of financial abundance and infinite wealth sound straightforward, and we hope that we've described them clearly enough for you at least to grasp them theoretically. What is not so easy is adopting and applying the attitudes we're describing. You may have to unravel many long-held opposing beliefs before you can fully embrace these new attitudes.

Becoming a wealthy person has to start with practicing a wealthier mindset. This is not something we are taught at school. So how are we expected to know how to do it?

Before we look at some of the key beliefs that you need to adopt in order to tune into the more money mindset let's get one thing crystal clear. No matter what the media tells you, no matter what your boss tells you, no matter what your yoga teacher tells you ... the world is not going to run out of money. *Ever!* Most of the money we use these days is virtual anyway. Furthermore, our major currencies are no longer tied to the gold standard. In fact, as of the time of writing (early 2014) no country in the world has its currency tied to the gold standard.

Be assured of one thing ... ***there is always going to be*** **more money**!

And so it follows that if the amount of money that exists in the world is infinite, then the amount of money you potentially have access to is also infinite.

Here are a few more concepts you need to embrace before you can be on your way to being infinitely wealthy.

Money is everywhere. You walk by opportunities every single day. The difference between you and wealthy people is that they took the opportunities they saw. If you are not taking these opportunities you need to ask yourself why. Maybe you don't trust yourself with that much money? Pay close attention to how you handle money. If you don't handle it well, change your practices. Psychologically, you won't trust yourself to handle more money until you're happy with how you handle the money you have. Most people run their businesses by holding onto money and then wonder why the business is not growing. You have to let money go to make more. You must be *ready* for a great opportunity to fall into your lap at anytime. If you're not ready, if you don't have the right mindset, then opportunities will simply pass you by because you're not ready to take them. Success happens when preparation meets opportunity. Don't worry if you've already missed a whole heap of opportunities, though; they come around every day and they keep coming. As soon as you *are* ready, you will suddenly see them everywhere, trust us!

The law of attraction. We've given the law of attraction a hard time up to this point in the book, but only because the concept has been so exploited and taken out of context. The law of attraction is, in fact, very powerful. It *is* true that the more you think about something the more it is likely to happen. In particular, the more you think about what you don't want, the more you seem to get it!

John: *I had a series of dead-end relationships and I couldn't figure out why I kept failing to find a good one. Finally I sat down and made a list of all the things I didn't want in a woman. I kept thinking about this list of qualities I* didn't *want. The next girl I met and dated . . . guess what? She turned out to have every quality on that list of things I* didn't want*! It wasn't until I made a list of the qualities I* did *want that I found someone who was perfect for me. The same applies to investing and business. Focus on what you* do *want (more money, smoother deals, good partnerships) and that's what you will get! Believe money will come to you in good ways and in great quantities*—truly *believe it—and once you take action, it will happen!*

Your perspective is your reality. Perspective is everything. Everything you see will be filtered through your mindset. Your perspective *is* your reality. If you don't like the way things are, change your mindset . . . sometimes that's the only thing you *can* change.

Tony Hsieh is a hugely successful entrepreneur and the CEO of Zappos, an online clothing and shoe company. At some point in the company's early days the board sent a marketing executive to India to see what the business opportunities were like there. He came back and said, "It's terrible. No opportunity at all. No one wears shoes there." A few months later the board sent a different marketing executive there. When he returned the board asked him what the business opportunities were like. "Fantastic," he said. "No one wears shoes there."

Here's another great story that shows how powerful perspective can be. There was a set of twin brothers who came from a very troubled and broken home. Their father was a violent alcoholic and their mother eventually left home, abandoning them. They were fostered by two different families and completely lost touch. Years later a journalist tracked them down and found that one brother had become a successful, wealthy banker, while the other brother had become an unemployed drunk who was always in trouble with the law. The journalist asked the latter brother, "How come you turned to a life of crime and ended up pretty destitute?" The man answered, "With a father like mine, what would you expect?" The journalist then asked the wealthy brother, "How come you became so successful and wealthy?" This brother also answered, "With a father like mine, what would you expect?"

It's amazing how two people can view the same situation so differently.

If you want to change your situation, you have to change your mindset.

John: *Don't forget that you also have the power to affect other people's perceptions through association. When I got an invitation to speak onstage along with Bill Clinton, my value shot up. People saw I was speaking in the same forum as Bill Clinton, so they perceived me as being on the same level as the ex-president of the United States! It gave me instant credibility. There is no way I'd be accepted onto a stage where Bill Clinton is speaking if I didn't know what I was talking about. When people heard I'd been on the same stage as Bill Clinton they believed they were getting guaranteed value when they chose to work with me, because they felt as if I had been endorsed by one of the world's most powerful leaders of all time. As you build your brand and expand your business one of your key objectives is to get endorsed by, and be associated with, highly successful people. If you're an author and you get an interview with*

Oprah, you might as well sit back and watch sales of your book go through the roof!

Now we hear you asking, "Isn't this more money mindset bordering on greed?"

Greed is about wanting more money for the sake of *having* more money. In contrast, wanting more money in order to have more freedom, more time with your family, and the ability to help others... how can that be greedy? It's a thirst to experience more of life, a passion to contribute more to the world, and a desire to redistribute wealth through generosity and altruism. Greed is wanting more than you *need.* There are always ways in which you can improve your life or the lives of others; so, while you might not *need* more chocolate or cake, you always *need* more money!

The Truth about Greed

We've been told:

Greed is bad. Wanting more is greedy.

The undesirable truth is:

The more you have, the more you can improve your life and the lives of others.

What do you remember from the story of little Oliver Twist? Probably that he asked for more gruel and was punished for it. The idea of wanting more is seen as a bad thing. If you think about the rest of the story, the man punishing Oliver—the evil manager of the workhouse—was actually the bad guy, and the story ends with Oliver being adopted by a wealthy benefactor who has plenty of money. So in the end Oliver does get more... he gets as much as he could ever want. Wealth wins in the end, and cruelty and meanness loses. But we're not often reminded of this part of the story; we just remember that he was punished for being greedy. People in Britain, right now, are being pushed and pushed by hard-sell advertising to give money to charity. "Three pounds will save a child's life today," they are told. "Text this word to this number and give £2 to rescue elephants from extinction." The people being coerced into doing this can barely afford to take care of themselves. They are struggling to pay their bills and feed their own children but are being emotionally bullied into giving to charity. Something is not right with that picture. The only people who should be giving to charity are those who have looked after themselves and their immediate families adequately. Charity begins at home. Only when everyone has enough at home should people begin giving to outside charities.

One of the practical ways in which we encourage people to develop a wealthier mindset is to think more about the value of something rather than its cost. We are too quick to ask what something is going to cost us, rather than asking what it is *worth* to us. Rather than ask, "How much will that cost?" we should ask, "What's the investment in this worth?" As soon as you think of something in terms of its cost, it's gone; it's been consumed. As soon as you start thinking of something in terms of its worth, you're looking at it as an investment.

You may be surprised by the number of ways that you can apply this technique. Let's take two examples: food and vacations.

You could go to the supermarket and spend £5 on fatty, salty snacks that have absolutely no nutritional benefits. You eat these quickly. They cost you money and your health pays a price too: Those snacks will have added a tiny extra layer of fat around your heart, causing a negative impact on your health. In this scenario, that £5 was a pure *cost* to you. Now think of spending that same £5 on some salmon and broccoli that you steam and eat with a portion of brown rice. The essential fatty acids and protein in the fish, and the vitamins in the broccoli, will help build your bones and enrich your brain cells, helping you when it comes to making some important decisions about a new business venture. In *this* scenario, that £5 was an *investment* in your health...and wealth (*you* being your greatest asset)!

You could look at the £500 you have to spend on a week's holiday in the same way. You could spend your £500 on an all-inclusive resort on the Costa del Sol, where you will be surrounded by other English people while you drink and eat as much as you can (to get your money's worth from that all-inclusive deal) and get sunburnt by the pool while you read the latest best-selling crime drama (with the same plot as the one you read last year). Alternatively, you could spend your £500 on a week of mountain climbing in the Swiss Alps, where you will increase your fitness, get the health benefits of the clean air, and maybe improve your German (which suddenly comes in handy when you get back to work and find there's a promotion up for grabs...for someone who speaks basic German!).

Another attitude that prevents people from adopting a wealthier mindset is that they harbor the notion that most success is born out of luck, which is a gross misconception. Even worse is the idea (that many mean-spirited, jealous people put about) that one person's luck can only come about at the expense of someone else's fortune. You can only think this if you believe the falsehood that there is only a finite amount of money in the world and that money is somehow a closed system in which you always have to rob Peter to pay Paul. We now know that this is *not true*!

Vince: *Chinese culture is full of superstition and stories with auspicious meanings. My father believes everything is down to luck. The Chinese believe that the person you choose to marry determines your fate in life; that choosing the right wife will make you lucky and choosing the wrong one will bring you bad luck. My father puts all my current success down to my choice of wife. My first one was unlucky; this one is lucky. Now, he has something of a point because my first wife was definitely a bad choice for me; we clashed terribly, we fought all the time, and life was very, very negative. It was a toxic environment that was not good for my health, my business decisions, or my general happiness. Compared to my second marriage it's like night and day. My wife, Annika, and I have a very harmonious relationship. It has been that way from the start, and that harmony has always helped me stay focused and positive and make good choices in other areas of my life. But I don't believe the wives I chose were random or have determined how lucky or unlucky I have been. My choices reflected how I felt about myself at the time. When I got married the first time I was not in a good place in myself, in my life. The second time things had really started to shift, and making a good choice about who I got into a relationship with and eventually married was a reflection of how my outlook had become much more positive and enriched.*

According to Felix Dennis, luck is just like love. It will come when you stop looking for it, when you're least expecting it. Your life is in your hands. You want to change it? Just do it. **Luck won't come and find you until you stop looking for it and start preparing for it.**

Taking Control of Your Money

It's fascinating how many people will entrust a virtual stranger with their money. It's *your* money so it's *your* responsibility. But so many people justify relinquishing all responsibility by saying things like, "I hate dealing with money, with investments, I'm just not good at understanding figures." Well... *get* good. It's not rocket science! Don't listen to the people who tell you that it's all too complicated. They are just looking to line their pockets by taking control of your money!

John: *When I was about 15, a man came to our door offering financial advice. My mother asked him in and told me to listen to him. He told me that if I gave him £40 a month for 10 years, I'd make a small fortune. So I listened to him and gave him £40 a month for 10 years. At the end of 10 years I got back almost exactly what I'd given him: no more and no less. Whatever he did with that money—whether he earned any interest on it or invested it and made a profit—I never knew anything about it. I could have put that money under my mattress and ended up with the same result. Or I could have invested it* myself. *Most financial planners are broke. They are usually looking for a way to use* your *money to line* their *pockets.*

The great father of modern economics, Adam Smith, said, "It is not from the benevolence of the butcher, the brewer, or the baker that we expect our dinner, but from their regard to their own self-interest." Do you really believe that people who offer to invest your money for you are concerned for your interests ahead of their own? Obviously their first priority is to make money for themselves. Did you feel sorry for Bernie Madoff's clients, or did you secretly think they were a little naive to trust him so implicitly with their money without asking too many questions about how he was allegedly getting such high profits from their investments?

The Truth about Your Investments

We've been told:
Let a (so-called) financial expert invest your money for you.
The undesirable truth is:
When you hand your money over to other people they are going to make sure they make a profit before you do. The best person to invest and take care of your money is you!

This one really makes us angry. As we've said before (and we will say again), the only reason other people want to invest your money is to make money for themselves. If they lose your money, you only have yourself to blame for giving up control of your investments. When you trust someone with your hard-earned money you are taking a massive risk. There are relatively safer risks to take. One is to spend a little money on educating yourself about investing. People who say, "But I haven't got time to learn about investments, I'd rather pay someone to do it for me," are basically saying they'd rather take a massive gamble than allocate some time to building future security.

It is your responsibility to look after your own money: If you don't learn how to invest your money, then you definitely don't deserve to have it and you may as well give it away.

Vince: *I always find it amazing that people will put all their faith in alleged business experts who present news stories on TV and/or publish their advice in national newspapers. These people are just journalists, doing a job for a salary of perhaps around £50,000 a year. If you want to learn to fly a plane you go learn from someone who flies a plane, not someone who writes about how planes fly. If you want to be a millionaire, go learn from someone who* is *a millionaire.*

Your Design for Life

Again, it is *your* life, and therefore it is *your* responsibility. If you don't know exactly who you are and exactly what you want, you will be what someone *else* wants you to be and you will want what someone *else* wants for you. Take a good look in the mirror and ask yourself, "What do I want?"

If you don't design your own life, someone else will design a life for you. What a waste of a potentially unique experience that is!

Everything is *your choice.* You may not *want* to be infinitely wealthy. If reading this book has made you decide that you *don't* want to be a millionaire (even if you agree that we all have a moral obligation to be as wealthy as possible in principle) because you are not comfortable doing what it takes to get there, then *great*! At least that is a choice. At least you have ventured into the unknown and explored the possibilities that are open to you instead of living like an automaton and accepting anything that other people impose upon you.

Not everyone does want to be a millionaire. Even those who say they want to be millionaires often don't really want to apply themselves and work to make it happen. They'd rather talk about what they'd do with a lot of money and keep buying lottery tickets. Ironically, many people who win millions on the lottery spend the whole lot in an alarmingly short space of time and end up worse off than they were before, and thoroughly depressed as a result. The worst thing of all is that they often end up completely unemployable because they've taken themselves out of the job market.

That's another reason the lottery is so dangerous. If you don't know *why* you want money and you are suddenly given it, you won't know what to do with it. You are likely to squander it just to relieve yourself of the burden of having it!

So…just in case you do accidently stumble across a million, wouldn't it be good to know exactly what you would do with it? Isn't it worth getting a little education on the subject of money?

Your Wealth Education

The journalist Ben Marlow wrote a fascinating article that appeared in *The Sunday Times* on 9 February 2014 about the number of young people who are choosing not to go to university in favour of taking a paid apprenticeship. Given the option of spending three years at university and racking up around £50,000 in debt while one of her peers secured a job and got paid to learn, Rosie Messiah-Harlock opted out of the university route. She got a Higher Apprenticeship in underwriting for a reputable insurance company and chose to earn while she learnt.

People are getting increasingly creative about how they get educated and what they want to study. The subject of wealth should be high on your agenda, especially if you have never studied money and finance in any shape or form.

John: *What we're seeing happen again and again is that A students end up working for C students. People who just studied and learnt what they were told to learn end up working for the big, successful entrepreneurs who dropped out but learnt the ropes of business the hard way. Many of Richard Branson's contemporaries who went on to obtain great academic qualifications probably ended up working for him 10 years later, earning modest salaries compared to Richard's millions (now billions!). The point is we can't all be brain surgeons because we don't all have the ability to gain the necessary academic qualifications. But most of us have the potential to become the next Richard Branson… if we're prepared to do the hard work.*

Vince: *I don't regret getting my university education or completing my MBA qualification. While I'm not actively and directly using what I learnt in either programme in my current work, I constantly use the analytical and research skills I learnt. However, I still feel that a formal education is oversold to people. There is nothing more valuable than the practical skills you can learn when you throw yourself into the deep end of a venture. If you can proceed to higher education, that's great, but if you can't for any reason you shouldn't be led to believe that this will hinder your success. You can't learn to* *do anything simply by reading books: There has to be an element of practice. You can't learn to drive a car by studying a manual on driving. Nor can you just get into a car and start driving without any instruction (or you'll end up having accidents and hurting people). You need to learn the basics of a skill, but then you need to get up and* do *it. It's the same with entrepreneurship. You can read a few books and take a course or two but in the end it is the* doing *of it that will sort the winners from the losers.*

The difference between British and American attitudes towards education is interesting. The Brits are not always so keen to pay for it, possibly because they see a good education as a right, given that traditionally the state has paid for all our education, all the way up to graduate level and beyond. Things have changed in Britain over the past 20 years or so, with loans mostly replacing grants for higher education, but the mindset is still there: Why should I pay for my education? In the United States, traditionally, people have always expected to pay for a college education: Either their parents have set aside money in a college fund or students have to take out loans.

Maybe people are more likely to value an education they have paid for themselves than one that has been handed to them on a plate.

Creativity is the key to being a successful entrepreneur. But you can't learn to be creative from reading about creativity in school. You can only learn creativity by *being* creative. There's a great scene in the film *Dead Poets Society* in which the maverick teacher, played by Robin Williams, tells his students to rip out the pages of a poetry manual. The teacher is ridiculing the idea that you can teach someone to write poetry in a step-by-step, methodical way. He believes the only way to write poetry is to put pen to paper and *write* it. When his students do this, they get amazing results.

The other thing you get when you acquire knowledge through doing something, rather than reading and learning the theory, is knowledge that is *unique.* No two people ever experience the same events in the same way, because we are all a complex combination of different thoughts and experiences. So when you gain knowledge through personal experience, it is your own *unique* knowledge . . . and that is a very valuable thing.

The more time and money you invest in learning, the more experience you will gain, and the more successful you will eventually become.

John: *The more you risk, the harder you will work. You have to have* skin in the game. *If you haven't put your money in, if you haven't invested and taken personal risk, you will play a different way. When I play poker with dummy chips I go all-in every time because I have nothing to lose. Then I learn nothing. When I play for real money with my own money I play a very different game and sometimes learn interesting new skills in the process. I believe I became a successful property investor because I sold my precious car and put all that money into starting my property business. I had everything to lose. So I worked harder than I'd ever worked in my life so I wouldn't lose!*

Vince: *I meet so many people who read and read and never* do *anything. You have to do both. I mentor a number of people and I impress upon them that they must read my course materials and then go out and do some real property deals. Half of my students read the materials religiously but never pluck up the courage to put the theories into action. The other half dive in without reading the course materials and then come back to me asking why their deals went wrong. The ones who follow what I teach (learn a little, then do a little) are the ones who are most successful. It's a balance. You learn the theory, then you put it into practice, then you look at your results and see where you might need to do things differently next time. Your results are your feedback. If you don't* do *the practice, you won't get the feedback. It's like doing a gym warm-up. You don't spend all your time warming up and never doing the workout, neither do you launch yourself straight into a vigorous workout. You do the warm-up, then the workout, and then repeat the next day.*

People often ask us why we teach . . .

John: *When people ask me why I teach, they often preface the question with "When you are so wealthy . . . " As in, "Why do you* need *to teach if you have a successful property business?" The answer is, I don't teach because I* need *to, I teach because I* want *to. I don't teach for the money, I teach because I feel that I have a duty to teach. If I have a lot of knowledge I think I have an obligation to share it with people, to help them avoid some of the mistakes I've made and to help them make more money than they could without that knowledge. If I know the easiest path to where the gold is buried and I don't point people in the right direction, I'm doing them a disservice. If I were head of marketing for a company and I knew of a marketing technique that would bring in thousands more customers and I didn't share it, I'd be doing the company a disservice. Keeping my knowledge to myself would be a disservice both to those who could learn from me and to those who have taught me. Of course my students are still not guaranteed an easy ride—but they may as well* *only have to deal with their own pitfalls and avoid the ones I discovered! I've made a lot of money from investing in property. I've also lost a lot of money investing in property. Why not tell others about the mistakes I made?*

Vince: *I feel a little differently about teaching. I'm not as altruistic as John about it! I don't feel obliged to teach and I don't feel it's my duty, as such, to share my knowledge with others . . . I simply enjoy it. I get a real buzz from teaching. Property development can be a lonely, frustrating game, with long hours spent going through paperwork and waiting by the phone for answers. I like spending a proportion of my time with people hungry for knowledge. I like the personal interaction with positive people who are eager to change their lives. Plus, it is a huge personal achievement for me to stand onstage in front of a big crowd and command their attention; I suffered from low self-confidence when I was a teenager, so I find it amazing that I'm now able to do this. I also firmly believe that we* learn *when we teach. By explaining something I know to people who were previously ignorant of it, I deepen and strengthen the knowledge I am imparting. But I also expect to be paid accordingly. I am saving people money by sharing my experiences and by telling them what not to do. If you have £300,000 to blow, and 15 years on your hands, then by all means go out and learn on the job. Or you can use a fraction of that money and invest a few hours of your time to hear about the mistakes I made!*

CHAPTER 13

A Foolproof Guide to Property Investing?

A little knowledge that acts is worth infinitely more than much knowledge that is idle.

—Khalil Gibran

Listen up, everyone...we are very excited to announce that we have a foolproof guide to property investing! Are you ready? Here it is:

Make money when you buy (i.e., buy properties below their market value so you're in profit from day one).

And as a special limited offer, while we have your attention, we are also giving away, absolutely free, the foolproof guide to losing weight! Ready? Here you go....

Eat less and exercise more.

The point we're trying to make here is that what sounds simple in theory is never easy in practice. If in one year you buy 10 properties that are valued at £100,000 each, and you buy each of them for £90,000, you automatically have a paper profit of £100,000. *Voilà!* A foolproof guide to property investing.

If you reduce your calorie intake by 10 percent and you increase your exercise by 10 percent, you will lose weight, as long as you do not have something medically wrong with you. *Voilà encore!* A foolproof guide to losing weight.

Okay, we didn't invent either formula; they've been around forever, but the fact is they are foolproof insofar as they definitely work.

What's the catch? Human intervention!

Value investing (and all we are doing here is applying value investing to property) is simple: Buy low, sell high. But people fail because they let their emotions get in the way: for example, they'll get a big tip about a stock and buy it despite the fact that it is overvalued, then become distraught when the tip doesn't pay off. Similarly, in the property market people get seduced by pretty houses and spend too much, then balk as the market dips a bit and they slip into negative equity. It's actually one of the biggest mistakes people make when getting into the property business: living vicariously through their business. They shop for pretty properties and fall in love with these properties. **The property is not important; the deal is important.** If it's a good deal (i.e., you are able to buy it at a decent percentage below its market value), then buy the property. If it's not a good deal, then don't. It's as simple as that.

The first thing to clarify is what property investing actually *is.* A lot of people call themselves property investors when they are really property *speculators* or property *developers.* All three titles technically apply to people who are *investing* in property, but we are very specific about what we mean by a **property investor**.

Property speculators buy properties at full market value with the hope of adding value through the appreciation of that property, thus making a profit *sometime in the future.* They may buy in an area that has been approved for a regeneration project or is already going through gentrification; perhaps a new high-speed rail link is being built nearby. Property speculators have to wait for the market to go up because of improvements to the area *before* the value of their property goes up and they can make a profit. Property speculation is very much a game for long-term investors.

Property developers buy properties that are run down or derelict, or have planning permission to be expanded, with the hope of adding value through improvements and renovations, thus making a profit *sometime in the future.* The speed with which they are able to do the work determines how quickly they can get that profit. They also need to ensure that their construction costs don't exceed the value they are adding. Of course, the longer they hold the property, the more it will hopefully appreciate in market value as well, but the principal goal is to *add value* by improving the property.

Property investors buy properties at below their market values so that they *are already in profit on the day they close the deal!* Property investors are not focused on making a profit sometime in the future (even though that might happen as well); they want to know that they have made a paper profit when they purchase the property by buying at a price that is lower than the market value of the property.

Of course speculators and developers can also be investors... if they also buy their speculative properties or renovation projects at below market value (using properties in comparable states for comparison). When you buy your derelict house, if you could turn around and sell it the next day at a profit without changing a thing, simply because its market value is more than what you paid for it, then you made a good investment regardless of whether you did any work. But for the purposes of what we are talking about in this book, property investors are simply people who *make money when they buy*, regardless of whether they are also developing or speculating.

How do you find a property and make a deal to buy it at below market value? That's the million-dollar (sometimes literally) question!

Warren Buffett, the guru of value investing, uses exactly the same principle when it comes to investing in stocks: He looks for those that are undervalued. He looks at the market value of a company and then at the price its shares are trading at. If he thinks that the shares are undervalued, he buys them. He doesn't get caught up in the hype of what something *might* be worth one day (speculation) and he doesn't buy shares in a failing company with the intention of putting in place managers who could turn the business around and raise its value (development); he simply buys stocks that he thinks are undervalued by considering the market value of that company *on that day*.

It makes sense to apply this tactic to buying property. But there's an even bigger advantage with property.

Property is the most leveraged investment you can make. The difference between buying stocks and investing in property is that you can borrow most of the money to buy property. If you want to invest £100,000 in stocks for the long term, you need to find that £100,000. If you want to buy a property for £100,000, all you need is £20,000—and you can more or less guarantee that the bank will lend you the rest. If the company you bought shares in went bust, you would lose your entire £100,000. If your house fell down or got blown away in a freak storm, you would only lose £20,000.

Additionally, say your shares increase in worth to £120,000. That means you've made a £20,000 profit, which is a 20 percent return on your investment (ROI). However, say your property increases in worth to £120,000. You've just made a 100 percent ROI.

Furthermore, with property you can *force* the appreciation. If you buy a two-bedroom house and turn it into a four-bedroom house, you've immediately added value to it.

Of course, stocks still have advantages over property (for one thing stocks are obviously more liquid) but no bank will lend you money long-term to invest in stocks. However, property is seen as such a safe investment that banks will lend you up to 90 percent of the value, and sometimes even more.

Even when there is a slump in the property market, you are better off investing in property than stocks. When the property market slows down people start to rent rather than buy, and the average price of rent goes up. It becomes a landlord's market. It doesn't even matter if you're temporarily in negative equity, because your rental income will still be coming in.

(*A note about negative equity*: In the case of a residential property the bank cannot force you to sell the property as long as you keep paying the mortgage repayments, even if you are in negative equity. The rules are slightly different for a commercial property; if you are in negative equity, the bank will ask you to increase your equity to maintain your loan-to-value ratio. Your loan can only represent a maximum percentagc of the value of the property [usually 80 percent]. For instance, if you bought the property for £100,000 with a £20,000 deposit, you'll have a mortgage of £80,000. If the property's value drops to £80,000, you must give the bank £16,000 so that you still have a 20 percent equity stake in the property. For this and many other reasons, commercial property investing is not for newbies!).

If you're looking for the best deals and the greatest profit from investing in property, the last place you want to look is in the estate agent's window. Estate agents are trying to sell properties for the *highest price* possible in order to maximize their fees—because most of them get a percentage of the selling price as their fee. A property investor is trying to buy properties at the *lowest price* possible in order to maximize their profit. If you want to get the best deals, you have to deal directly with people. This is why we always emphasize to our students that property investing is a *people* business. You have to be good, or *get* good, at dealing with people. You need to be confident and good at networking. You have to learn good negotiating skills.

Don't confuse *market value* with *asking price*. The asking price is what the estate agent has set and is a fairly arbitrary figure. Estate agents are forever pushing up asking prices. They know they are rarely going to get the full asking price (although they love using the line "We're starting to see many properties going for our full asking price" to entice potential clients!), so they often overvalue properties to hedge their bets. Sellers sometimes get a nasty shock if an estate agent has managed to get the asking price out of a buyer but the valuation from the buyer's mortgage company comes in under that price. When this happens, either the seller must drop the price or the buyer has to come up with more cash to make up the difference (in which case the buyer has paid above market value for the property).

The *market value* is what a surveyor provides. But even that number is based on many arbitrary measures. Once a surveyor has established that there are no major structural issues, the only measure of value is what similar properties in the area have sold for. The market value is based on supply and demand, as long as the market is efficient. During a property bubble—a time of dynamic growth—or a major property slump, determining the market value becomes more and more difficult for surveyors.

Estate agents love a property bubble: The higher the prices go, the higher are the commissions they make. As a property investor, you don't actually want a property bubble because prices rise too quickly and sellers get greedy. You earn more money with a steady rise in the market. If the market rises too quickly, it will come down quickly. This is what happens when people speculate.

Too high a level of property speculation usually causes a property bubble. This is currently taking place in Asia. Everyone knows that property prices in Asia are on the rapid rise, so everyone is trying to get a piece of the action, with the result that asking prices are becoming unrealistically inflated. Eventually the property bubble will burst and anyone who bought at the top of the market will lose out.

In the end, of course, a property is only worth what someone is willing to pay for it.

Ultimately, a property investor is looking for a motivated seller who will accept a below-market-value offer for the property in exchange for the convenience of a quick transaction with no middlemen and no chain (where the purchase of a property is dependent on the sale of another, which in turn may be dependent on the sale of another property and so on). For many sellers the nightmare of a long chain may rear its ugly head more than once. This happens more regularly with properties in a higher price bracket. If you ask people who have experienced a chain breaking (i.e., someone in the chain pulling out, meaning that no one else in the chain can complete their sales), they will tell you it is one of the most frustrating things they have ever experienced. They often have to start the whole process of marketing their houses again, not to mention the extra money it costs them in mortgage repayments while they hold onto their properties for another few months looking for new buyers, or replacements for the people who dropped out of the chain are found.

The Golden Rules

Here are our golden rules for property investing, no matter what market you are buying, selling, and renting in.

Golden Rule 1

Only deal with motivated sellers. Unless your seller is highly motivated to sell, you won't get the best deal. It's as simple as that. Anyone who needs to sell quickly and is interested in a chain-free cash buyer is a motivated seller. A motivated seller's reasons for needing a quick sale range from being under threat of repossession to last-minute emigration. What they want is a guaranteed sale by a certain date, and they are often willing to give a discount on the market value for that guarantee.

Golden Rule 2

Deal directly with the seller as much as you can. When you deal with an agent or an auctioneer, you only get to negotiate on *price*. What enables you to get the best deal is the ability to negotiate the *terms*, and you can only do that directly with the seller. For example, say I find a motivated seller who needs to sell in two months. He wants £170,000 and his property is worth £200,000. I can offer to pay him £140,000 now and a further £30,000 in 5 to 10 years, by which time my equity in the property should have increased. I'll share some of my profits with him in the future so I can get a better deal now. He gets a guaranteed sale now. I can only negotiate this deal directly with the seller.

Golden Rule 3

Always make money when you buy a property. Don't buy a property unless you will be making an immediate paper profit by having agreed to a deal with the seller that allows you to buy the property at **below market value** (BMV). If you are not going to realize an immediate paper profit the minute the deal is completed through buying at below market value, you are speculating rather than value investing.

Golden Rule 4

Always do your due diligence. If you don't uncover every stone, you could come across something that costs you dearly in the long run.

Golden Rule 5

Only buy where there is rental demand. You *must* think about rental potential. You need a good catchment area for renters. It's no good buying property in the middle of nowhere.

Golden Rule 6

Get in for as little as possible and get your money out as fast as possible. Always put down as little money as possible. You are looking to *control* the property, not have a chunk of money tied up in it. As soon as you have a sizeable chunk of equity in your property, get it out as fast as you can so you use your profits to buy more property. Keep your money working for you. A good place to start is to release some of the equity in your home and use it as a deposit for your first investment property. If you are sitting on equity in your own home, it is not making a good return on investment for you. If the bank is loaning you money on your mortgage at a rate of 5 percent and you take that money and invest in something giving you a 20 percent return, you are making 15 percent. Why pay off a low-interest loan when you can use it to make a higher return elsewhere?

Golden Rule 7

You must play the numbers game. You need to talk to at least three to five motivated sellers a week to increase the odds of finding a good deal. Many investors are passive. They sit around waiting for the estate agent to call. But they could literally wait forever. And in any case, if the deal was that good, why would the estate agent call you rather than calling a personal friend or taking the deal themselves? The deals they'll call about will tend to be the tricky ones, deals that often come with hidden catches. And the pressure from the fear that the estate agent won't call you again if you don't take the deal may sway you into taking that problematic deal. The only way to maximize your chances of getting the best deal is to find motivated sellers yourself, speak to them directly to ensure the deals are genuine, and select the best opportunities.

Golden Rule 8

Don't wait to buy property, buy property and wait. If your goal is to become a property millionaire, you need to start as quickly as possible. A property worth £100,000 is going to take a very long time to become a property worth £1,000,000. However, if you buy 10 properties that are each worth £100,000 (for a total portfolio value of £1,000,000) for £20,000 equity in each (for a total net asset value of £200,000 with mortgages totalling £800,000), and if each of those properties doubles in value in 10 years (it actually takes an average of just over 7 years for properties to double in value), then your total portfolio value would be £2,000,000 at that point but your mortgages—assuming they were interest only—would still only be £800,000. Thus, **your net asset value would be £1.2 million**.

Going back to Golden Rule 2: If you are not clear on what we mean by a below-market-value deal, here's a very simple hypothetical example of someone making a BMV deal with a motivated seller.

Jane knows a wealthy property investor; she met him at a networking event for property investors. They talked about working together. The investor has money but little free time, while Jane has time on her hands but no cash to invest, so she offers to be on the lookout for leads. One day Jane happens to hear that her widowed neighbour, Margaret, is desperate to sell her house and move to Canada, where her daughter has just had a baby. Margaret's house, which she owns outright, is worth £100,000, but Jane gets Margaret to agree to sell for £80,000 on the condition that the deal will go through in four weeks. Jane has just made a deal worth £20,000 on paper. She goes to her investor, who has £80,000 in liquid cash, and offers to *sell* or *flip* this deal to the investor in exchange for a £5,000 fee. The investor makes an immediate paper profit of £15,000, Jane makes £5,000, and Margaret gets a lump sum of £80,000 for her retirement plans in Canada. Everyone's happy.

Most people (thanks to all the property programmes on TV) think *flipping* means to buy a run-down property and do it up, and then sell it on. This is certainly a form of flipping a property, but technically *flipping* encompasses any deal (in the form of an agreement) that is *sold on* by the deal maker to another party, such as a cash investor. The deal maker does not have to complete a transaction; an agreement on paper is enough for the investor to buy the property. (In the United States, *flipping* is a much looser term and simply means that a property is bought and sold again in under six months.)

Programmes like *Property Ladder* got a lot of people thinking that developing (or the U.S. notion of flipping) property is easy and that anyone can do it. But unless you have great DIY skills, you are probably opening a massive can of worms that could cost you more money than you bargained for. You are much better off finding a BMV deal and flipping it to an investor—or a developer if the property needs work—than getting involved in construction work yourself. Why work any harder than making a deal?

While we're on the subject: We advise people who are serious about investing **not** to watch property programmes. They distort reality. You watch Kevin McCloud follow a couple building their dream house from scratch in *Grand Designs* and the *perception* is that they have done it within the hour you were watching! Of course, you know that isn't the reality, but it's a powerful experience that detracts from the truth . . . which is that it took them five years!

In the same way, programmes like *Homes Under the Hammer* make people think it's easy to make money at auctions.

This is not always the case!

Auctions: Caveat Emptor

Many first-time investors automatically gravitate to auctions. Obviously they assume that this is where the best deals can be made. In theory, this is what you would expect, but in practice it can be a very different story.

If you want to buy a property at auction, make sure you read *all* the small print, check out the property beforehand (*don't* buy blind unless you can afford to gamble with your money) and remember *caveat emptor* (buyer beware!). This means that it is the *buyer*'s responsibility to ensure she knows everything about what she is buying at an auction.

Auctions should only really be the domain of experienced property investors. For anyone else they are simply a gamble. No matter how they look on TV, auctions are not a safe place for the first-time investor.

Vince: *I made some good deals at auctions initially. I probably did my first seven or eight deals on properties I bought at auction. However, I had some experiences, and heard of some experiences, that eventually put me off them. I came to the conclusion that there was always a reason a property was at auction, and it usually didn't favour the buyer. Either the property was at auction because there was something wrong with it and it had proved difficult to sell through estate agents, or it was at auction because it was a special property and the owner wanted to gamble that he could get more money (*above *the market value) by creating a bidding war on auction day. Neither is likely to be a property that you want if you are an investor.*

What some inexperienced investors don't realize is that your auction bid is binding: You can't easily walk away if you change your mind. I knew someone who bought a property without checking it out first. After the auction this person discovered that the property had a huge structural problem so the lender refused to approve the necessary mortgage. Another woman I knew bid on something and won the bidding. Later she had to admit that she didn't have the deposit in place. She had to pay hefty fines to get out of the deal. I myself once incurred a massive bill after winning a bid on a property, because I didn't know all the leaseholders in the building where the property was located had agreed to spend a huge amount of money having some work done on the roof and common areas. As the new owner of the flat, I was obliged to pay my share.

When I look back, I realize I actually got very lucky with my early successes. In truth, I probably got a little bigheaded about my knack of getting good deals at auctions. I soon learnt that pride comes before a fall!

Shortly after Annika and I were married, we invited her parents over from Denmark to spend some time with us in our new home in Milton Keynes. I had earmarked a property in London that I wanted to buy at auction. It was a studio flat in Camden Town with a guide price of £110,000. However, other flats in the area were going for much more. I'd had it valued at £185,000 so I knew I had an instant £65,000 paper profit if I could get it close to the guide price. Of course, I knew I'd probably have to go above the £110,000, but to me, anything up to about £160,000 (giving me a paper profit of £25,000 or more) was worth it. I was prepared to go up to £160,000. I was very excited. I wanted to show off as well. I wanted to show my new in-laws that they had this fabulously wealthy and flashy property investor for a son-in-law. Maybe I deserved my downfall!

The night before the auction we all went up to London and spent the night in a fancy hotel. We got to the auction very early the next morning. I anxiously waited for my lot to come up. I tried to be all cool and laid back but I was sweating buckets. I so desperately wanted to impress my wife and her parents. By the time my lot came up, I was trying to stop myself shaking. The room was packed. The auctioneer called the lot and asked for someone to start the bidding. No one made a move. I waited. I certainly wasn't going to be the first to bid. He waited and then asked again. The room was silent. You could have heard a pin drop. This seemed to go on forever. Just as I was wondering whether I was going to have to make an opening bid, a voice called out, loudly, from the back. "Two hundred thousand," a guy shouted. I couldn't believe my ears. £200,000?! Even if you are prepared to go that high, you don't start the bidding at that price when no one's made a peep. It was all over. No one was prepared to go over that price (obviously!) and we all sloped out of the room. I had never been so embarrassed in my life. I was livid. That idiot, whoever he was, had not only had a very odd approach to auction protocol but had stolen all my thunder. I walked out of the room unable to speak, I was so furious. It took me a long time to get over the embarrassment and disappointment.

Learn before You Earn

Before you start investing in property, you *must* learn the ropes. Imagine you have L plates on, like a learner driver. Don't worry, you'll get to take them off, but you must psychologically wear them to begin with, to remind *yourself*, as much as anyone else, that you are still in learning mode.

Once you feel you've gained enough knowledge and experience, you can take the L plates off and *learn* will become *earn*!

People perceive the property business as having very low barriers to entry, in that anyone can get into it. This is true, but it still doesn't mean it's easy or that you don't need to educate yourself first. Mistakes in property investment can be cripplingly costly!

Vince: *I remember a woman coming to me because she'd inherited £50,000. She wanted to start investing in property. She was interested in taking my course and learning about property investing. At the last minute she pulled out because she said she'd found a portfolio of properties that she could just invest her full £50,000 into through a lease-option deal. I advised against it. I told her she would be better off investing some of that money in educating herself before taking the plunge. But she ignored my advice and went ahead and did the deal. She thought it was a good deal because it was a portfolio of tenanted properties. Several months later she called me in tears saying that she had found out, after doing the deal, that 80 percent of the tenants had given notice, and that there were substantial structural repairs needed on most of the properties. I asked her what her option period was. She didn't even know. At that point there was little I could do to help her, other than to be a shoulder to cry on! You* **must do your due diligence***. Nothing is as costly as ignorance.*

To become a successful property investor you don't just need to learn about the ins and outs of the property business, you need skills that will allow you to find, contact and negotiate with sellers. Those are the skills that will eventually set you apart from others, and take you forward to expand your business and your brand. Property may not ultimately be the business you want to build—the business that represents your *passion*—but it can *fund* your business and eventually enable you to build your brand. It will certainly give you great transferable skills!

Anything you learn in life is valuable.

You never stop learning. *We* never stop learning.

The property industry is forever moving and shifting. Trends come and go, and tactics that worked 10, 5, even 2 years ago do not necessarily work as well now. The fluctuations in market prices are only one changing element. Access to information opens up exponentially as the Internet becomes increasingly sophisticated. Legislation changes, loopholes close, new ones open up; you have to be on your toes and endlessly vigilant to keep up and ensure you get the best deals. If we could see where the next lucrative loophole was going to open up, we'd jump on it in a heartbeat. Who knows, maybe *you* will find it; maybe you will be the one who makes the next big sweep. But you'd have to be in the game. You won't find it by lurking around on the outside. You need to get in, learn, keep going, make mistakes, keep going, have some successes, keep going and maybe you'll crack something new.

The legendary ice hockey player Wayne Gretzky once said, "A good hockey player plays where the puck is. A great hockey player plays where the puck is *going* to be." (He also said, "You miss 100 percent of the shots you don't take.") And here's a great example of that philosophy. In the heat of the social media and smartphone application explosion, two Stamford students turned a craze on its head. They created an app called Snapchat. The software allows users to take photos and record messages that they can send out to recipients who have a small window in which to view them before the messages are *deleted forever*! In June 2013 their company was valued at $800,000. Six months later Evan Spiegel, one of the company's cofounders, reportedly turned down an offer of $3 billion from Facebook; a month later, he turned down $4 billion from China's Tencent Holdings. That's called catching the next big wave!

Vince: *Back in the early days, when I first started, I used to drive around to properties to view them. I don't do that anymore. I can get enough information to make a deal from questioning the seller and doing my due diligence online and over the phone. I can literally do a deal from my bedroom! Furthermore, I can figure out what needs to be done in order to get the property let out. I have letting agents who will go and view the property and let me know what needs to be done and how much rental income I can expect to achieve. I have so many rental properties that I now have a central lettings manager who liaises with all the local lettings agents to oversee maintenance of the properties. I don't really want to know if a boiler is broken or if there's a blocked drain. Unless there is a major problem that is going to require an extensive investment, I just let my staff get on with it. If you want to be successful, you have to delegate, and you have to learn to trust people to service your business!*

John: *I have been endlessly creative in my marketing tactics throughout my time as a property investor. I remember once putting an ad in a local paper saying, "We buy ugly houses." It worked! I'm not necessarily looking for curb appeal. I've bought a handful of rather attractive properties—there's one in the Lake District that I'd consider living in myself—but for the most part my properties have been dumps that people are desperate to get rid of. That's how I've managed to buy so many properties at below market value. I buy them and do what needs to be done to make them rentable. Renters are not as fussy as buyers. They don't mind living in an ugly house because they know it's a temporary accommodation.*

One property trend that backfired as the bubble burst was the big high-rise apartment blocks that were sold off-plan. Many people lost money on these. Developers bought land on which they planned to build high-rise apartment blocks (theoretically an extremely good use of land indeed, as the higher you go, the more money you can make per square foot of land). They hugely inflated the price of the apartments after seducing people with swanky show flats with high specs (that were usually available for a premium on top of the basic price) and then explained how buyers were getting a huge discount by buying off-plan. Of course, once the apartments were finished and buyers had shelled out the full amount in the expectation they would be able to start charging a huge rental income, the dream shattered. The majority of these apartments stood empty, costing their owners a fortune in mortgage payments because the apartments weren't as popular with renters as the investors believed they would be. The fact is, traditionally we haven't lived in apartments in this country. Brits generally live in houses, with gardens. Even in our major cities, the appeal of a one-bedroom converted Victorian garden flat far exceeds the appeal of a tenth-floor luxury apartment that wouldn't look out of place in Tokyo or Singapore.

Many of those swanky high-rise developments still remain half empty today, with the real market value of the apartments being far less than what the owners bought them for. They cost many investors dearly.

Vince: *At the time of writing we are seeing a similar scenario take place in Malaysia, where John and I are often invited to give seminars on property investing. They are approaching the top of a highly precarious property bubble due to speculative developers selling properties off-plan at inflated prices. We are urging people to be cautious, but they are queuing up around the block to get these properties. They are* bragging *about how much they are paying for properties; it's nuts! We've urged them to look back at what happened in the UK, but only a fraction of these people seem to be taking heed of our advice. It will be interesting to watch what happens in the next few years over there.*

Deal Making

We are forever reminding our students that it's not about the property; it's always about the deal.

Furthermore, the deal is less about the price and more about the terms. The terms are what make you a unique buyer. If you have offered the seller favourable terms that someone else can't, then even if someone else comes along and offers her the same price she is more likely to stick with you. Again, it's a people business and the point of doing business directly with the owner—in other words, cutting out the middle man, the estate agent—is so that you can focus on the terms and get creative.

Doing a property deal is a complex process and you can't afford to skip any steps. It's like baking a cake. If you left out one ingredient (the eggs, the flour, etc.) or skipped a step (creaming the butter, perhaps) or you put it in the oven at the wrong temperature or baked it for the wrong amount of time, the cake would be ruined. The same logic applies to doing property deals.

So let's take a look at the basic steps of finding and making a property deal.

Leads. You cannot even begin to negotiate a deal until you have found a motivated seller who is interested in doing business with you. You find those motivated sellers by sourcing leads. You get leads from doing your marketing and ensuring that your service is the first one people will think to turn to when they need to make a quick deal. Estate agents are not the place to get deals. If a property is being marketed by an estate agent, it's unlikely that the seller is motivated enough. In any case, the seller will have to make enough on the deal to pay the agent's fees and commission, which leaves less in the pot for you to negotiate for. Estate agents do not often market the properties of highly motivated sellers; if there was a good enough deal to be made, the agents would probably have done a deal with the seller themselves. There are a number of ways of finding leads, ranging from an Internet marketing campaign to leafleting, but you have to follow up every potential lead. Remember our Golden Rule 7: If you're not talking to at least three to five motivated sellers a week, you're not really in the game. It's a numbers game. The more people you speak to, the more chances you have of one of them turning into a deal.

Identifying a motivated seller. What makes someone a motivated seller? You must find out in order to be in the best negotiating position. There are several reasons why someone might need to sell as quickly as possible and be willing to take a

BMV offer in exchange for a quick, guaranteed transaction. It's not only people whose properties are being repossessed who are in need of a quick, guaranteed sale. It could be a couple going through a divorce or a couple getting married who need to combine their assets to move to a new property. Maybe a new baby is coming and a family is desperate to move to a bigger place before the birth; they've found their perfect property, but the buyer for their current house has dropped out. Sometimes you might save the day by being a so-called **chain angel**—someone who comes in to save the day when a chain has broken. If your seller isn't highly motivated don't waste your time, because you won't have the best negotiating position.

Financing strategies. You have to know how you are going to finance your deal before you go in to negotiate. If you don't have your own money to invest, you need to have an investor willing to take the deal with the terms that you are able to negotiate. If you need a mortgage, you need to have your mortgage broker at the end of the phone. You must have all your ducks in a row before you go in to negotiate.

Negotiation. Many people think they are great at negotiating but fall apart when they are put to the test. Negotiating skills are very specific. There are many psychological nuances, both conscious and unconscious, that can make or break a negotiation. You have to know exactly what you are selling before you start. So what are you selling? You are selling the property seller a *solution*. When we teach negotiation skills, we pick students to make live calls to prospective leads. Many of them suddenly dry up in the middle of the call and one of our team has to take over so we won't lose the deal. It's not as easy as it looks. You are in a powerful position when you speak to sellers and offer them a way forward. And, as Spider-Man knows . . . with great power comes great responsibility! So you really need to know what you are doing before you dive in. You have to become an expert negotiator. Once you've established that the seller is genuinely motivated, you can make your offer, which will hopefully lead to making a lockout agreement. Of course, all your initial offers are subject to a surveyor's valuation.

The lockout agreement. You should never move forward until you have a lockout agreement with the seller. This is an agreement giving you the exclusive right *but no obligation* to buy the property at the agreed price within three months. Even if you have agreed to push it through faster than that, you need that three-month window as a contingency in case any unforeseen delays occur. If a search doesn't come back in time or if there are leasehold issues, you need that protection so that you don't lose the deal. It is basically a short option agreement.

Legal work. You must ensure that you have all the necessary legal paperwork in order. You need a solicitor to do your side of the paperwork, but the seller needs a solicitor, too, or the deal could be challenged in court if anything goes wrong. Your solicitor should be poised to push through all the necessary searches and gathering of information as soon as you get your lockout agreement signed.

Valuation. Once your lockout agreement is signed, you will instruct a surveyor (at your expense of course) to make an official valuation of the property. This is obviously a make-or-break point because if the valuation comes back lower than the market value that you based your offer on, your deal will become null and void, and you'll need to renegotiate.

Renegotiation. Your offer is always a percentage below an agreed market value. If the seller has stated that the property is worth £150,000 and your offer is 25 percent below that value (i.e., £112,500), the offer is only valid if the surveyor's valuation is £150,000. If the surveyor comes back with a figure of £140,000, then the original deal is off. You can always make a new offer to the seller, but it will be based on the new valuation. In this case, for example, you would go back and offer £105,000 (25 percent below £140,000).

Mortgage offer. If a mortgage is going to be necessary to complete the deal, your mortgage broker should be ready to push it through as soon as the valuation has come in and the deal is confirmed.

Releasing funds. Whether the purchase of the property is being financed through a mortgage or a bridging loan, it is your responsibility to ensure there is no hold up on this front.

Completing the deal. There should always be a mutually agreed-upon completion date for the deal, which could be absolutely critical when dealing with some sellers, especially if they have mortgage arrears that must be cleared.

The deal can fall apart at any time. The seller can go AWOL, the financing can fall through, the valuation can come back well under what you were expecting: A whole list of things can go wrong. You have to keep your wits about you; it's a juggling act and you have to keep all your balls in the air at the same time.

Look at all the different elements that go into making a property deal: It would be an uphill climb to become an expert in all of them. This is why property investors often team up. One person may be particularly good at finding leads while another is great at negotiating. Network, and partner up with people who have skills you lack while you offer them the skills you do have. When you form partnerships you also spread the responsibility. If you know your niche, what you are best at, you can take responsibility for it, while someone else focuses on a different aspect of the deal. You can trust that someone is out there finding leads while you are negotiating deals and someone else is reading all the small print, making sure the deal is watertight.

We teach people every step of the process, from finding leads and negotiating deals to troubleshooting problems to ensure that the deal goes through. We also provide a turnkey service so that if people want to bring us leads we can negotiate the whole deal from start to finish. We can do the whole thing, or various parts of it, for a sliding scale of fees.

John: *I advise people never to put all their money into one house. If you have all your equity in one house, your money is not working for you. If you spread it over 10 houses, you are maximizing your investment potential because you are maximizing your leverage. However, there is a tipping point. If you have too many mortgages and too many liabilities you become a risk to the bank. When you have £1 million leveraged on one or two houses, the bank knows that it can easily call in the debt. When you have between £10 and £20 million leveraged, the bank knows it would be extremely difficult to call it all in. You become a problem to the bank because you have negotiating power; you could negotiate the terms of paying the loans back. With a loan of £1 million on one property, the bank has most of the power; with £10 million leveraged on several properties,* you *have the balance of power. It's a position* *that the banks will try to avoid getting into. This doesn't mean you are broke or bankrupt. Remember, your net asset value (NAV) is your total assets minus your total liabilities. If you own 40 houses worth £250,000 each and you have a £200,000 mortgage on each of them, your assets total £10 million and your liabilities total £8 million. Your NAV would be £2 million, but it would be very difficult to liquidate all your assets in a hurry. Therefore the bank sees you as a liability.*

Vince: *The bigger your portfolio, the more you spread your own risk. If you own 10 houses and 2 of them are vacant because you haven't found tenants for them, it's not the end of the world. If you own three houses and two are empty, you're in bad shape! If you want to be a successful property investor, you need a business mindset; you need to think of your portfolio as a business. I see so many investors with the small-time mindset of a landlord. They get very focused on one or two properties and on doing all the maintenance work themselves (thinking they are saving money by not hiring people), but this is not a good use of their time. If you were the CEO of a company, you wouldn't go round fixing the photocopiers to save money on engineers! If you're serious about property investing, you need to look at it as a business and make good business decisions by maximising the time you spend on making your money work for you, and delegating the more menial jobs to appropriate contractors.*

Don't forget about appreciation when you're looking at the size of your portfolio. The bigger it is, the more your capital will appreciate. The amount of your mortgage is decreasing (as long as you are paying off some of the capital) while the value of your property is increasing. If your NAV is currently £2 million, in 7 to 8 years it will probably be around £4 million (going by trendsover the past 50 years).

The Truth about Your Mortgage

We've been told:

Work hard for 25 years to pay off your mortgage and be debt-free.

The undesirable truth is:

Debts secured on appreciating assets are good debts. When your money is stuck as equity in a property, it is not working for you.

Most people are not taught the difference between **good debt** and **bad debt**, or they believe the distinction is too complicated to understand. But it's really very

(continued)

simple. Bad debt is debt secured on something that is depreciating in value. A car loan is bad debt because the minute you drive your car out of the showroom it begins to lose value. Credit card debt is the worst kind of bad debt as it is secured on nothing, because the things you've bought with it—such as food and holidays—have probably been consumed! But a loan secured on assets that appreciate in value, such as property, a business, government bonds and commodities, or perhaps artwork, is good debt. If you buy your house outright and there is £200,000 of equity in it, that money is inactive. That money could be better placed as the deposit on four other houses that pay you rent. Think of the game of Monopoly . . . do you want one hotel on Park Lane, or a whole row of houses along several streets and a couple of utility companies over which to spread your investments?

Ultimately, property is not about ownership, it's about control. If you live in your home and have a 100 percent mortgage on it, what is the difference between you and your neighbour who is renting his home from a landlord? The answer is control. You don't *own* your home any more than your neighbour does. The landlord owns your neighbour's home, and the bank owns yours, but the difference is . . . **control**. *You* can hang a picture on the wall or paint your bedroom pink if you want. *You* can install a cat flap or a waste disposal unit. Your neighbour can't do anything without first getting permission from the landlord. Plus, if you live in your house for 10 years, the amount it has appreciated in value is yours to keep. Your neighbour's capital appreciation belongs to the landlord.

Vince: *Property is the best way of getting your money working for you. Asset building is the fundamental way to borrow and save for the future. At the time of writing, we have just seen the government put into place policies that—once again—are designed to inflate the property market. The help-to-buy schemes introduced by Chancellor George Osbourne in 2013 will most likely lead to another bubble that will eventually burst . . . and so the cycle goes on! But I still say to people, "Take whatever you are offered." If you see an opportunity to invest in property—at the right level—then take it. It's the only investment for which the banks will lend you a huge amount of money. You put in a relatively small amount of money to control a huge asset. It is always, ultimately, going to be advantageous to you. However, it is still a long-term gain and you have to ensure you do not become asset rich and cash poor. You* *must do whatever you can—whether it is getting a rental income or trading the financial markets—to get a decent passive income as cash flow to live off while your assets appreciate. If you can't do that,* at least *get some money into appreciable assets. Remember, if all you have are debts and liabilities, you are financially worthless.*

It doesn't even need to be your money: As long as you have some control over an appreciable asset you are on the right path. So look at every conceivable way of getting that control. Which brings us nicely to . . . lease options!

Lease Options

This is such a huge topic it requires more specialized study to come to grips completely with all the ins and outs, but we can give you an overview here.

Vince: *I was the first property investor in the UK to get lease options for residential property legalized. I had heard of how the concept worked with commercial property and couldn't see any reason why it couldn't be a creative way of doing residential property deals. I met with a lot of resistance but I pushed through and succeeded in getting it legalized. I've helped countless people in several countries profit from property deals by using lease options.*

So let me give you a little history on my background in property investing, and show you how I stumbled across the idea of using lease options to buy property.

When I first decided to invest in property, I went in blindly, finding deals any way I could: through estate agents, at auctions, and by going directly to sellers without agents who advertised in local papers. I had some ups and downs, some successes and failures. I did my fair share of refurbishments as well . . . with mixed results. After a few years I was getting a little frustrated and jaded. Shortly after the auction nightmare with the Camden Town studio that I mentioned earlier, when I didn't even get the chance to bid on a property I'd had my eye on, I decided I had to find a different way of sourcing properties to buy. That auction experience showed me just how much time and money could be wasted in sourcing and researching property deals that come to nothing.

I took a long, hard look at my skills and experiences. This was around the same time I folded my Internet site, WamBamBoo.com. I was disappointed it had failed, but I had already realized I was walking away with excellent transferable skills. I knew I was great at marketing (I just needed a better positioned business to market). Also, with all my experience as a pharmacist, I knew I was a compassionate people person. And I'd learnt a number of good business skills studying for my MBA. I just needed to figure out how to combine and monetize my skill set to best effect. I eventually came up with the idea of creating a network of sellers. I created a database of thousands of motivated sellers and made a lot of money by charging people for access to them. With some of the leads, I negotiated deals that I then flipped to another investor; with others, I made an offer myself and added the property to my own property portfolio.

I had gathered the most important commodity in the property investment business: the names and addresses of qualified *motivated sellers. (By qualified, I mean that I had a filter system that asked specific questions to ensure that the seller was truly motivated. My system asked them questions about their circumstances—sometimes asking them an important question twice in an are-you-sure secondary question—to ascertain that they were truly motivated to sell as quickly as possible.)*

I soon became well known throughout the industry as the expert in lead generation.

To date, I have had over 100,000 sellers contact me. I am known as the guy who can get people's houses sold regardless of their situations or the condition of the properties. People who have little experience with the property business assume that when people want to sell a house, they make it all pretty inside then go to an estate agent who takes pictures that are displayed in the window and eventually, after fielding a few offers, the house gets sold for a good price. This is a completely idealized scenario; not everyone has the ability to follow this pattern.

Sellers go through all kinds of problems. Their houses sit on the market for ages, they have buyers pull out, they need to move quickly or get the equity out of the property quickly, or maybe the property has been left to them by a deceased family member and is in bad condition but they don't have the money to do the work. Sellers can have any number of reasons why they need a quick, direct sale. I created a service that virtually guaranteed people a sale.

At the time I launched my new property business, it was relatively easy to get financing and make money by making below-market deals. As John described before, you could simply buy a house at a discount and immediately refinance it for more than you bought it for, giving you an instant cash profit. The banks soon closed this loophole and these days you have to wait six months before you can refinance, but you still make a paper profit when you make a BMV deal.

Just to review how this works . . . say a house is worth £100,000. The most the bank would lend me to buy that property is £85,000. Technically, I need £15,000 of my own money for a deposit. What I actually do is offer the seller

£80,000. The seller agrees and the deal is struck. I take that agreed deal and show it to a cash investor who agrees to lend me the £80,000 at a high interest rate so I don't have to apply for a mortgage. I can go straight back to the seller with the cash and close the deal. As soon as the deal goes through, I refinance the house, getting a mortgage for £85,000, which allows me to pay back my loan with the interest I owed. I now own a house with £15,000 equity in it, without having used any of my own money.

I literally did hundreds of deals. Again, some I didn't even complete myself; I just flipped them for between £5,000 and £7,000. (John bought around 35 properties using this technique back in 2007 and 2008.)

As I explained, with all the tightening of the rules after the financial crash, the banks have made it harder to refinance, but the honeymoon period was great while it lasted!

What goes up must come down. We'd had 11 years of sustained growth under the Labour government. I'd watched the property market grow and grow and I knew the bubble was going to burst. Property prices were due a correction. Sure enough, this started in early 2008 when the market started its nosedive. With prices falling rapidly, it was much harder to get any below-market-value deals, because the sellers' equity was being eroded. They were at risk of getting nothing back or even owing the bank money on their properties, which could have taken them down the road to bankruptcy.

As things got worse, I put my thinking hat on and tried to come up with another solution. I've always believed that ***when you help others, you help yourself****, so by keeping my focus on how I could help financially troubled homeowners sell their properties, I was also looking for a way in which I would benefit, as the buyer.*

As prices slumped and the recession kicked in, people lost their jobs, leaving them unable to make their mortgage repayments. As I watched this happen, I realized that many people were in real jeopardy of losing their homes. As a property investor, you are looking to make money in two ways—from a monthly income as well as from the appreciation in the property's value—so it makes sense to build a large portfolio of properties at the bottom of a property slump. How could I combine these factors to help myself and help struggling property owners?

Lease options seemed like a great answer.

Here's how lease options work: I take over someone's mortgage payments while leaving the property in the owner's name, and simultaneously make a deal that gives me the option to buy the property in a number of years' time at a price agreed on today. Everyone gets a good deal. By my taking over the mortgage for a certain number of years, the seller is relieved of that responsibility. I can then rent out the property for a profit. I have an option—which means I have the right *but no* obligation*—to buy the property at a certain date, and as the price is set several years before that date, the difference between the price I pay at the time I exercise my option and the value of the property is the money I make in appreciation.*

The deal I just described is not about ownership; it's about control. *Even when you own property in the traditional way with a mortgage, you don't actually own it; the bank owns it and you just control it . . . as long as you keep up your mortgage repayments. When you grasp this concept, it's easy to get creative with property investing.*

Lease options give the investor control even without having to transfer ownership.

When I first suggested the idea of using lease options *to control property at investor forums, no one believed it would work. People pointed out that it wasn't even legal to use lease options for residential property. But I only saw the benefits for both investors and sellers, especially those who were getting into negative equity. I stood my ground and worked tirelessly to get the process legalized using an expert commercial property lawyer, and once I did I never looked back. It's far less time consuming and stressful than pushing through the process of purchasing the house and dealing with all the eleventh-hour paperwork that usually rears its ugly head! It's a much more efficient way of ensuring that people don't lose their properties through repossession. In some cases we were able to work out a deal for the owners to stay on as tenants (although John had one particularly bad experience in doing this, as he will describe in the next chapter!).*

At the time of writing, I am working with regulators in Holland to get lease options legalized there. The situation for property owners in Holland is much worse than it is here. Many people are in negative equity and at the moment it is technically illegal for them to rent out their property to cover the mortgage. Tenanted properties are seen as an extreme risk because tenants have far more rights than they do in the UK. There's no short-hold tenancy agreement in Holland as there is in Britain. Once tenants are in, they basically have the right to stay there as long as they keep paying rent! Conveyancing in Holland is done by a notary rather than a solicitor. I am working with a number of notaries to try to get lease options legalized. It's an uphill struggle. The Dutch banks are monopolistic and are fighting hard against us. There is a regulator, but the banks are being very resistant. It's like a David and Goliath battle but I'm determined not to give up.

I remain a real advocate of lease options; I think it's a great win-win situation for both buyer and seller in the right circumstances. In fact, the property I currently live in with my family is under a lease-option deal. I have the no-obligation option to buy it from the owners in eight years' time. I currently pay them a premium rent, plus *I take care of the maintenance of the property as if it were my own. This gives me the control to do whatever I want to the property and to live any way I like in it. I can even make improvements that add value to the property, which will benefit me when my option to buy comes around. The property is currently worth £1.3 million. It's a difficult property to value as it's the only property of its size and type in the Northamptonshire village where it's located, but it will definitely increase in value after eight years and the amount by which it has appreciated will be my capital gain. The current owners get premium rent with none of the usual responsibilities of landlords, and I get to look after my future investment with the option to pull out if for any reason something goes drastically wrong with the property or the market. It's win-win however you look at it.*

People before Property

We've said it before and we'll say it again: The property business is a people business, so you need excellent people skills. Whether it's the sellers, the solicitors, or your investment partners, you are dealing with people at every step of the way. Knowing how to deal with people is therefore a key skill you must acquire and hone.

Because of the low barriers to entry in property investing, almost everyone assumes they can throw some money down, buy a few houses and rent them out for a nice passive income. But it takes a lot more than that. Yes, it is a meritocracy (i.e., anyone can do it), but property investing comes with a huge amount of responsibility.

People often come to us because they have made mistakes and lost money trying their hand at property investing without educating themselves first. We show them how much money they could have saved if they had learnt some key skills before diving in.

Property investing is perceived as being a glamorous business. People want to get into it because they picture themselves as property tycoons, buying up beautiful mansions and calling themselves property millionaires. We aim to give them a more realistic picture.

Vince: *I'm actually in the property business for the people, not for the properties. It's the people who make it exciting, interesting and rewarding. I have always been motivated by the idea of helping people. This goes right back to my days as a pharmacist. The sellers who contact me are often pretty desperate. I do everything I can to help them. Even if it turns out that I can't, I will tell them about IVAs (individual voluntary agreements) or refer them to a debt management service. Executing an IVA often means that they won't be able to borrow for a few years, but that's better than total bankruptcy. The property business is a tough business to be in. The uneducated attitudes can be particularly galling. There is a common belief that cash investors are trying to exploit people by offering low prices, but nothing could be further from the truth. Cash investors are offering desperate sellers a solution when no one else can. Of course there is a payoff. Sellers are relieved of their burden; they get a fast, secure deal and we get a profit. The BBC once interviewed me on this subject, and I was adamant that it is not exploitative to help people who urgently need to get their money out of their properties or be relieved of the burden of mortgage repayments. It's like payday loans, which are now getting a bad reputation. If people need to borrow money to eat and heat their houses, what other options have they got? If the government can't help them, and their friends and family can't help them, they have to go to someone who can.*

One of the most touching stories I remember was a widow who called me and said she wanted to sell her house as fast as possible. She hadn't been able to sleep even a night in it since her husband had died. They'd lived in the house for over 50 years until his death. The house was dated but immaculate inside, and lovingly cared for. I'm sure many estate agents would have seen pound signs in front of their eyes and done a big marketing campaign to get the most money they could for the house, but all this woman wanted was to sell the house as fast as possible. The house was worth £150,000; I offered her £120,000 and we completed the deal in four weeks. I made an instant paper profit, and she had a nice lump sum with which to buy a small apartment, rebuild her life, and enjoy her retirement. She was extremely grateful.

I believe I probably have had more experience in dealing with sellers than anyone else in the business. I have dealt with thousands and thousands of sellers in the course of my career. I have built a reputation for being an expert at talking to motivated sellers. And where did I get my people skills? From being a pharmacist and talking to a countless number of people about their ailments and problems. I developed a way of speaking compassionately to people with problems and finding a way to help them. Again, the property business is not about the properties*; it's about the* people *who own them. It's a people business; people's circumstances matter. The more you get to know people, the* *more you understand what they need and the easier it is to do a deal with them. When you buy through estate agents or at auctions, you don't get to deal directly with the sellers. It makes all the difference in the world to be able to talk directly to the people who ultimately make the decisions.*

Once again . . . a property is not an inanimate object; it is an extension of the person who owns or controls it. The property business is a *people* business, and that's why you must invest in learning *people skills.*

CHAPTER 14

Property Investment in Practice

All things are difficult before they are easy.

—Thomas Fuller

We've always felt that the best way to teach people is to share our experiences with them, so in this chapter we're going to share with you some of our firsthand experiences in property investing. You'll see how it's a rollercoaster of highs and lows. You win some, you lose some . . . and you never know what might be lurking around the corner. All you can do is keep your wits about you, do what you believe is best, and take it on the chin when things don't work out the way you hoped!

John's Property Stories

Let's start with a good one!

Paradise in the Lakes

One of the most positive experiences I ever had took place in 2008, when I was contacted by a guy in the Lake District who was struggling to sell his four-bedroom bungalow. It was in an area where a major industrial plant had been shut down. The guy had lost his job and needed to relocate with his family to an area where he could find employment using his specialized skills. The problem was hundreds of ex-employees from this plant were in the same situation, and properties were simply not moving. He'd had a couple of offers that he'd accepted, but both times the chain had broken. This is quite common with properties of that size, especially when something like a mass redundancy triggers a big upheaval.

The guy was pretty desperate by the time he called me.

Up until this point I had only ever bought properties that were in a very poor state. I had a big portfolio, with properties all over the country. I had bought in Manchester, Guildford, Derbyshire, Luton, Biggleswade, Leeds and Liverpool, as well as in Wales and Scotland, to name but a few familiar places, but all of those properties had been badly kept or were located on run-down streets. These properties were damp, smelly, needed work, and in general were places you wouldn't have even let your pets sleep in. I'd seen things you probably couldn't imagine. I'd bought a property from a guy who'd let his dog urinate and defecate all over the house. I'd seen places that looked and smelled as if they hadn't been cleaned in several years. I'd had to have the most disgusting messes cleared out and cleaned up before putting a property on the rental market. Before I went to see that house in the Lake District, I'd never purchased a property that I'd actually be happy to live in myself, so when I saw it I was pleasantly surprised.

The house had been on the market for a while with an asking price of £325,000. I offered the guy £250,000. He accepted my offer and I drove up the same day to get the paperwork signed. It was still light outside when I arrived that evening. I pulled up at the bottom of the drive, where there was a beautiful old country pub. I'll never forget getting out of my car and looking up at the house that was sitting on top of a hill. It looked beautiful. It was set in the middle of one of England's most picturesque rural areas, the Lake District. When I finally entered the house, the interior didn't disappoint me either. It was a well-cared for house, nicely appointed, with spacious rooms. Okay, it was a bungalow, which worked against it since bungalows are not particularly popular in England—they tend to be associated with elderly or disabled people who need their houses to be step-free—but it was a lovely home; I could easily have lived there myself.

Was I scared that I'd struggle to sell it someday, as this seller had struggled? No. By that point in my career I'd had enough experience to trust that I could sell—and rent out—any property, in any condition. It all comes down to price and terms. I do not believe that there is an unsellable or unrentable property. You just have to keep adjusting price and terms, and looking for the right customer. I've got all the tried and tested strategies at my fingertips!

I signed the deal with the guy that very evening and we completed the transaction within four weeks.

For this seller, I was a chain angel, someone who wasn't in a vulnerable chain, a cash buyer who could make a deal quickly, a deal that was not subject to the sale of another property. As the saying goes, "A bird in the hand is worth two in the bush." The guy was too relieved to have a guaranteed sale to worry about accepting an offer below the market value; he'd already had to find a way of covering several months' mortgage payments without an income. He was happy to get rid of the responsibility of the property and the mortgage on it.

For me, it was a great deal. I eventually got the property valued at £305,000 and I was able to take out a 90 percent mortgage on it for £274,000—but I had only paid £250,000. The day I bought that house I made a £24,000 profit, *on top* of the £31,000 in equity I now had in the property. The mortgage was at a very low interest rate. It was during the era of subprime mortgages and I had a mortgage broker who knew all the best deals. Of course we now know that the subprime mortgage market undermined the global financial markets and partly caused their crash, but at the time you just took advantage of whatever was on offer.

The Lake District property was a great investment in a really nice property, I hardly had to do any work on it and it was easy to find tenants for it. My monthly mortgage payment was around £900, and I managed to rent it out for £1,200, so I ended up with a passive income of £300 a month from that property.

The house was definitely a step above all my other properties. The day the Lake District property deal went through, I felt like I'd just moved up a solid rung on the property investment ladder.

The Cannabis Factory

I do believe that some properties are cursed! One of my most bizarre stories began when I got wind of a property for sale in a Merseyside town sometime around the end of 2009. It was an unusual property in that it was a four-bedroom detached house with an annex. It was just off the motorway. The sellers were relocating imminently and they were getting desperate to make a quick sale.

I spoke to the seller on the phone before I went to look at the property. He told me it was on the market for £275,000. I explained that I usually offered around 20 to 30 percent below the asking price. This meant I was probably going to make him an offer of £200,000.

The first mistake I made (which almost cost me the deal) was to phone an estate agent I knew in the area. I told him the address of the property and asked him if he knew it, and if he knew of any issues with it. He said he knew the property because he'd once marketed it and they'd accepted a couple of offers that had eventually fallen through. Stupidly, I told this estate agent that I had offered the guy £200,000 and was confident of making a deal with him.

I turned up to view the property and make a deal with the seller. While I was talking to him there was a knock on the door; it was the estate agent I'd called. He'd turned up to try to talk the seller into selling the property to *him*! Fortunately the seller told the estate agent to go away as he was making a deal with me. So I ended up buying a four-bedroom house with an annex that was worth £275,000 for £200,000. Not a bad deal. And one that almost slipped through my fingers because someone tried to go behind my back and pull the deal out from under me.

But that's not the end of the story.

It's amazing what you learn when you break your own rules. We've all done it. We set our boundaries and stick to our principles, until the day that we don't. The day we let down our guard and *make an exception*. Nine times out of ten, it backfires and reinforces why we set our limits in the first place.

I started marketing the house on the rental market as soon as I made the deal, but I wasn't getting any bites. A couple of months went by with zero interest. There was nothing wrong with the house, and I even lowered the rent a couple of times, but I just wasn't getting any bites. Finally I decided to advertise it on Gumtree, a big national notice board site that advertises properties for rent and sale, jobs, cars for sale, services, and so on. I was contacted by a couple who said they were very interested in renting the house. I met with them to show them around and they said it was perfect for them. They were a Chinese couple who had just moved to the UK. As such, the guy told me they didn't have any references or proof of income, but they had cash. I told him I never normally considered renters without references, but that if he paid six months' rent up front, I would relax my conditions. I guess I identified with him and understood his predicament. I knew Chinese people who had moved over to the UK and had struggled to get their lives going because they didn't have bank accounts or references. But most of the Chinese people I knew in this position had money, and the guy said he would have no problem paying me cash up front for six months' worth of rent, so I had no reason to believe anything was untoward. The guy drove a BMW, and he and his girlfriend were very well dressed and presentable; there were no obvious red flags.

So I took the money and gave the couple the keys to the house.

Three months later, I tried to contact the couple to make a house check. I tried calling the house and their mobile phones, but there was no answer and they never returned my calls. I went around to the house and put a letter through the door, asking them to contact me to arrange a time for an inspection. No response. Of course, legally I have to get the owner's permission before entering the property, but I was getting seriously worried. I drove over to the property and knocked on the door. There was no reply. All the curtains were closed, and what really worried me was that there was a broken window. It was just a small hole but I couldn't think why they wouldn't have contacted me to get it fixed. Finally I decided that because I'd tried to enter the property by going about it the right way but had had absolutely no response from them, I was within my rights to let myself in. I tried my key in the door... but it didn't work. They had changed the locks! Now I was growing extremely concerned.

I left the property and the next day, while I was in another location on business, I called a local builder who often worked for me and asked him to go round to the house with a locksmith and try to get in and take a look around. I'll never forget the moment I got his call later that afternoon. I asked him if they'd managed to get in to the house and if everything was okay. He said it definitely wasn't okay, but he wouldn't tell me why over the phone; he just told me to get round there immediately.

I jumped in my car and drove straight round to the property, my heart thumping in my throat. When I got there and joined my builder inside, I couldn't believe my eyes. The front room was like a jungle. It was completely filled with green leafy plants. There was an elaborate sprinkler system affixed to the ceiling. There were large ventilation ducts running throughout the house and huge holes had been knocked through the walls and ceilings to accommodate them. The entire house had been torn up to create a huge cannabis factory.

Obviously I called the police immediately. They never tracked down the Chinese couple.

But that's *still* not the end of the story of this house.

My builder gave me a quote of £30,000 to fix the damage. I didn't want to spend that kind of money, as it would have seriously reduced the profit I'd made on the place, so I got creative. On finding out that the house was now empty, one of the neighbours contacted me to say that he was looking for a house for his son and daughter-in-law to rent. His son happened to be a builder, so I made a deal with the couple. In exchange for fixing up the property and repairing all the damage, they could rent the house from me with an option to buy it at an agreed price after seven years. It was like giving them a mortgage they couldn't get on their own. They would rent from me, fix up the house as if it were their own, and then if they wanted to buy the house after seven years they'd have the option to do that at a price that had been fixed seven years earlier, allowing them to acquire any equity from appreciation. This was a basic lease option deal. I had my initial investment protected, plus the monthly rental income. I even offered to deduct their construction expenses off the rent if they gave me itemised receipts for everything they spent. They supplied their labour for free because they were living in the house, and I got a house repaired without paying for the labour.

And there's one more twist.

Before the seven years were up, the couple broke up and the guy handed me his notice. He didn't want to exercise his option to buy the house. Was that a wise decision by him? Probably not, because he could have continued renting, bought the house from me as agreed, and then immediately sold it again, probably for a profit, but he was in low spirits due to the breakup of his marriage and he just wanted to get rid of it.

So (finally) the end of the story is, I got back a house that had been renovated at minimal cost to me, plus I was able to rent it out again in its renewed pristine condition.

My Professional Tenant

In some ways this story is even worse than that of the cannabis factory, for reasons I will explain.

I remember this day as if it were yesterday. I was driving through Manchester, quite close to where I was living at the time, on the way to see a friend. It was late 2009, a few weeks before Christmas. I was in my silver BMW, which had an in-car system that alerted me when I got texts and read them out to me. A text came in from a guy who had found my contact details on my website. It included his address and postcode. It caught my attention because it was a Manchester postcode. I replayed the message; the name of the road sounded very familiar. I was sure I knew it. At that exact moment in time, I was driving down the main road and my instinct told me to take a right. I had a hunch that this was the road. I was right; it was the road the guy had just mentioned.

I called the guy and he picked up the phone. He asked if we could meet and talk about his situation because he was desperate to sell his house. I said I was close to the area (I didn't say I was coincidentally parked on his street; I thought that might look a bit weird and stalker-ish!). He asked if I could come over in half an hour.

I waited in my car for half an hour and then drove up to his house, parked and knocked on the door. I sat with the guy and his wife in their kitchen for over an hour while he told me his story. He'd been made redundant from his job a few months before. He'd got into arrears on his mortgage, which turned out to be one of the worst types of subprime mortgages that were around at the time, with an interest rate of 12 percent. Worst of all, it was a few weeks away from the anniversary of the death of one of his children. It was a very sad story and I felt sorry for the family.

I explained to the guy that I could buy his house and let him live there and rent it back from me. He'd been paying over £900 a month for his mortgage, which was ridiculously high for a house that was worth £100,000. I said I'd rent it back to him for £500 a month (in line with the going rate for that sized property in the area). I knew he'd be able to manage that amount with the help of Housing Benefit until he got a job.

I knew I wasn't going to make much of a profit. By the time I'd paid the mortgage I'd taken out on it (at a more reasonable 4 percent, which gave me repayments of about £450) and my insurance, I barely broke even. But I wanted to help this guy and his family. It sounded as if he was going to get back on his feet; he'd just hit some hard times. It was what I specialized in at the time, helping people avoid repossession and eviction. Through creative financing, I was in the position to help the family stay in their home, whereas all the mortgage lender wanted to do was to get them out. This lender had given a guy a mortgage at a horrendous interest rate (this was happening all the time before the crash) and when the guy failed to make his payments, the lender was within its rights to take the property back. No one was going to hold the lender responsible for lending at such a high rate to this guy; it was totally legal, but was it fair or responsible? I felt that it wasn't entirely, which is why I wanted to step in and help in these kinds of situations.

So I paid off the arrears, bought the property and waited for the guy to pay his rent, which he did the first month... but not the second, or the third. He paid some the following month, and then came up with excuses the month after that. I would go round there and he'd pull on my heartstrings again with another sob story. He'd tried to get a job but figured out he'd lose his Housing Benefit. He'd worked out that he would actually be better off, financially, if he stayed unemployed. He said he was just catching up with some bills and he would have all the back rent for me very soon.

The lesson I was beginning to learn was this: the nicer you are to people, the more they will take advantage of you.

I'm sure you can more or less guess how this story goes. After a few more months the guy stopped paying his rent altogether. I called him regularly, but all I did was try to reason with him; maybe that's why he took me for a fool. I never threatened him; I just kept reminding him that he owed me a lot of money. But after a while I couldn't even get hold of him. After 12 months of missed payments (while I had to continue paying the mortgage), I was desperate to know what to do. I joined an online landlord's forum to try and get some advice. I explained my situation and people came up with a whole list of ideas, ranging from sending the heavies round to going round to the house and waiting there until he came home to talk to him. One person suggested serving an eviction notice. In the end, that's what I did.

A court date was set and I assumed that I'd get my house back pretty fast. But when I turned up in court, the judge asked me for a rent schedule. I didn't have one. I had a contract with the guy, stating the amount of rent that was due each month, and I had proof of when he *had* paid me. But I had no proof of when he *hadn't* paid me. I was supposed to have a separate document outlining every date rent was due, and when it had and hadn't been paid. The judge postponed the hearing and set another date. I had to wait several more months before we went back to court. This time I provided a rent schedule, but it was a new judge and my tenant had a very clever solicitor. I'm still not sure how they managed it, but the guy was given more time to come up with the rent and wasn't evicted. I think it was because he said something along the lines of, "I didn't really want to sell him my house, but John talked me into it." This just left me reeling; I'd saved him from being repossessed! He was a classic professional tenant—someone who had figured out all the loopholes of how to stay in a property without paying for it.

Finally, I was telling someone my story one day and this person recommended a very good solicitors' firm that specialized in these types of cases. I went to them, paid them the £2,500 fee they asked for, and three months later the guy was out of my house. A condition of the agreement was that I couldn't go after him for back rent, but I didn't care by that point; I just wanted my house back. But I couldn't believe how the whole episode had unfolded. This man and his family had lived in my house for free for almost three years. I was out of pocket for around £30,000. The irony is that all I ever wanted to do was help this guy out—while adding a small property to my portfolio. I'd worked so hard to help the guy avoid repossession and eviction...and in the end I'd been forced to evict him myself!

With hindsight, what I should have done is gone straight to the specialist solicitor as soon as the guy stopped paying, paid my £2,500 and had the guy evicted. I would have saved myself a fortune. But this was the very treatment that the mortgage lender had threatened him with, that I felt was so harsh and was trying to spare him from. This is the downside of getting too compassionate in business.

The reason this case felt so much worse than the cannabis factory was that this guy had blatantly abused my good nature. I took it as a personal affront. The couple that got away with turning my house into the cannabis factory for six months pulled a fast one on me, but they could have done it to anyone, and it was my stupid mistake for accepting them as tenants with no references. Plus, I got the house repaired for next to nothing and it all worked out in the end. This guy just took my goodwill and stamped all over it. And it all cost me £30,000. It was an expensive lesson, and one I wouldn't wish on any of you.

£100,000 from One Phone Call

The professional tenant isn't my only experience with difficult tenants, but the next story ends up a little more favourably for me!

While I was a member of a property networking group, I was approached by another member of the group one day, after I'd spoken on stage about my experiences. She had a lead she didn't want because the situation seemed like too much trouble, but she thought I might want it. The property was in Aldershot, not far from where I lived at the time, in Guildford. It was owned outright by a woman who lived in Derbyshire and she was desperate to get rid of it. The problem was that she had extremely difficult and abusive tenants who were in huge rent arrears and were not taking care of the property. Similar properties on the street were valued at between £175,000 and £190,000. The property in question had been on the market for years but the owner hadn't managed to sell it because of all the problems associated with it. No one wanted to take on those tenants. I was working with an investment partner at the time and we decided to make an offer. I remember sitting in the car with my partner and calling the owner on the speakerphone. We offered her £85,000. We said that was the maximum we were prepared to pay for the house, but that we could do a fast completion. We made the offer and then waited. The line went dead for what felt like an eternity. We began to think she'd simply hung up, but eventually she said, "Alright then." I couldn't believe it. Yes, it was a huge headache cleaning up the property after the tenants left (we were lucky they left of their own accord when the property changed hands), but two months later we sold the property for £185,000. Before costs, we'd made £100,000! This was exactly the type of property we used to go after—a problem property. If someone has that much equity in a property but can't release it, she may as well take a massive reduction on the selling price for the peace of mind she gets from relieving herself of the responsibility. This Derbyshire woman didn't technically make a loss because she probably bought the property years ago for a fraction of the price she sold it for, and had paid off the mortgage on it. To her, it was £85,000 in her pocket and no more stress. She was very, very happy. So were we!

Vince's Property Stories

At Her Majesty's Pleasure

In early 2009 my sister Florence, who is one of the key members of my team, took a call from a woman who was desperate to sell her house.

Her circumstances were rather extreme, even compared to all the crazy stories I'd heard in my time.

The seller explained to us that her husband had gone to jail for a series of violent crimes. She couldn't afford to keep up the mortgage payments on the house. She wanted to sell, get the equity out of the house, and move herself and the kids in with her relatives while she regrouped and decided what to do next. She wanted to sell as soon as possible.

I made the woman an offer she was happy with and we were all set to do the deal, but one thing stood in our way: The property was in joint names and I had to get the husband to agree to the deal too. The woman and her husband were not on speaking terms so I had to write to the prison and request permission to speak to him. I don't know whether you've ever tried to talk to someone in prison—especially in a hurry—but it's not that straightforward! I finally got permission to speak to the guy. At first he wanted nothing to do with the deal, but I talked him around and we came to an agreement. He agreed on the condition that the deal went through quickly. However, we ran into a few holdups due to local searches and other administrative problems, so the deal didn't move as fast as I'd promised. And this is how I got my first (and only, thankfully) death threat! The guy started threatening me that if the deal didn't go through he'd come and kill me when he got out. Never mind motivated sellers . . . this experience turned me into a *very* motivated buyer! Thankfully we did eventually complete the deal and the woman got her money . . . and I lived to tell the tale! She was extremely grateful and we were all very relieved when it was over.

We told you property investment was not for the faint-hearted!

My Paranoid Seller

We keep saying that the property business is a people business. As such, you get to deal with the good, the bad, and the ugly; and as we specifically deal with highly motivated sellers, we are more often than not dealing with people who have fallen on difficult times or who are in extreme circumstances. (Some of these people seem to be in these situations through no fault of their own but with others you have to wonder.)

At some point in 2006, Florence took a call from a woman in Liverpool who said she was desperate to sell her flat because she had broken up with her partner and wanted to get out of the area and start a new life elsewhere. Florence listened to this woman's story, which seemed to go on forever. The woman went into great detail about how terrible her ex was and why she had to get away as soon as possible. She said the flat was worth £90,000; Florence explained that we generally offered around 18 to 20 percent below the market value, which would mean an offer in the region of £70,000. The woman agreed to this and Florence started doing her due diligence.

Florence's research on comparable recently sold properties in the area confirmed that the flat was indeed worth around £90,000, so she called the woman to confirm our offer of £70,000 subject to a surveyor's valuation. The woman broke down in tears, crying and telling Florence that she was being followed. Florence asked her if she'd contacted the police. She said she hadn't because she had no proof, but she was absolutely sure that she was being followed everywhere she went and was even being watched in her own home. It all sounded very odd. Florence eventually brought the conversation back to the flat and our offer, and the woman expressed her gratitude effusively.

Half an hour later, the woman called back and completely changed her tune. Florence said it was like talking to a totally different person. The woman started screaming at Florence, calling her a crook and accusing us of trying to cheat her out of her flat and con her into taking a terrible deal. Florence was very taken aback and explained that the woman had contacted *us*, not the other way around, and that if she wasn't interested in selling she didn't need to sign the paperwork, she was free to walk away. The woman hung up, but then called back a little while later to say that she'd calmed down and was just stressed because of being followed; she reiterated that she was absolutely desperate to move. She said she needed more time to think about the deal we were offering and Florence said that was absolutely fine, she could take as much time as she liked.

For a couple of weeks, the woman went back and forth like this: one minute calling up and shouting abuse down the phone, the next minute telling us she was almost ready to sign and was desperate to get out. Eventually she said she was definitely ready, and Florence sent her all the paperwork to sign; the deal giving us the option to buy the property at the agreed price. Once everything was signed we sent out our surveyor, which changed everything.

Our surveyor came back with information that was completely new to us. He discovered that the woman had put the property up for auction with a guide price of £70,000, but that it had failed to sell. Who knows why it failed to sell, maybe the woman had set too high a reserve on it, but regardless of the reason it meant that the surveyor couldn't value it at more than £70,000.

There was no way that Florence could have uncovered this information in advance unless the seller had provided it (which she should have done). These days, with all the advanced searches you can do online and the range of websites dedicated to the property business, it's easy to get information on when and where a property has been offered for sale, but back in 2006 only a surveyor could access information about auctions. The open-access websites that tracked property sales at that time only gave limited information about properties that had been sold.

Florence had to call the owner to say that the property had been down valued to £70,000, meaning our deal was off. The highest offer we could make was 20 percent below the valuation, which would be less than £50,000. Obviously it was impossible for the woman to accept that figure as it wouldn't even pay off her mortgage. I'm sure you can imagine her reaction!

This is another example of the huge risk associated with auctions. If you put your property up for sale at a certain guide price and it doesn't sell, this information goes on your property's record and the guide price will be factored into any future valuation. Not a lot of people know that!

Your property has a reputation, just as a person has a reputation. Any repossession order, eviction notice, failure to sell at auction, and the like is noted and may affect the valuation. Many newbies would not be aware of this. We certainly weren't when we started.

Furthermore, in the UK and throughout Europe, if a lender doesn't get all its money back when a house is repossessed, the lender can actually go after the seller for the difference. In the United States this is illegal, which is why many American owners just walk away from properties and leave the keys in the door when they can't keep up with their mortgages and are facing repossession. In the UK lenders can actually bankrupt owners by going after them for shortfalls if the lenders don't make what is outstanding on the mortgages when selling the properties. Repossession followed by bankruptcy was a sad reality for many people in the UK after the financial crash.

The One with a Happy Ending

To end on a positive note, let me share with you a story that *does* have a happy ending!

I remember a call we got from a woman in 2008. She was in a terrible state. She had been made redundant about six or seven months earlier and had got into arrears on her mortgage. For some reason she had missed the cut-off date to apply for redundancy compensation. She thought the compensation was going to wipe out her mortgage arrears and was devastated when she found out she hadn't qualified because she had missed the deadline to apply. She lived in a nice three-bedroom house with her adult son who didn't work due to a disability, so she was supporting her son as well as trying to keep her house going. She had obviously been in heavy denial about her situation, not believing that the bank would ever actually throw her out. When her arrears hit £3,000 she got her final warning and was informed that the bank had been able to get a repossession order. Unbelievably, she was calling us two weeks before the date that the bailiffs were due to arrive.

This is a familiar story to us. People often go right up to the wire. They are suffering from shock and depression when they are in arrears and being threatened with losing their home. They bury their heads in the sand and stop opening letters, hoping they will wake up from the nightmare. But this is serious stuff. Mortgage payments have to be made; there are no two ways about it.

This woman, however, was the most extreme case we'd ever had. We literally had two weeks in which to get a deal in place. Anyone who has bought a house knows that conveyancing is a lengthy business, and two weeks is no time at all in which to get it done. It was all eleventh-hour stuff. In the end we got everything together and the deal went through at midday of the day that the bailiffs were due to arrive later in the afternoon. We were lucky to get the repossession order suspended because we had only exchanged contracts that day. Some judges are strict and want to see that all the arrears have been cleared before they will lift the repossession order. We got a lenient judge who was satisfied by the letter from our solicitor saying that contracts had been exchanged.

When I tell this story to people, I'm often asked if it wouldn't have been simpler and more straightforward to have let the bank repossess the property and then have made our offer to the bank directly, since banks are usually willing to take a discount on the market value of a property as long as they get their money back. But banks are not that easy to deal with. When you are dealing with the bank, you are dealing with an organization that cares only about the money and not the actual property. Dealing with the seller gives you a lot more room for negotiation around the terms of the deal. Plus, as I said above, you don't really want a repossession order on the house's record. A house that has been repossessed automatically loses a little value; it's like the house gets a bad credit report, in the same way a person can get a bad credit report. It's unfair, really, as it's not the house that's at fault but the owner, but that's how it is.

* * *

We hope that through telling some of our stories we've reinforced the point that it's never about just the property—it's much more about the person who owns the property and his or her particular story. Get good at understanding and dealing with people, and you'll be on your way to becoming a successful property investor!

> A life spent making mistakes is not only more honourable, but more useful than a life spent doing nothing.
>
> —George Bernard Shaw

CHAPTER 15

Being a Wealth Dragon

You are never too old to set another goal or to dream a new dream.
—C. S. Lewis

Top 10 Wealth Dragon Principles

We have so many principles that we believe you need to adopt if you want to be a wealth dragon, but these are the 10 that we feel are the most important to follow.

1. Make a Commitment and Light Your Fire!

So many people live in a kind of fog. They're happy to go with the flow and stay in a rut because they're not really ready to commit to what they want. Often they are not even sure what they want. But once you *do* know what you want, you have to make a firm choice to go after it. And when you've made that commitment you need to get fired up about it or else nothing will happen. Get excited. Get motivated. Take action. You can't do what it takes until you are *committed* and *passionate* and *motivated*! Most people spend their lives wishing for things. They wish they had more time with their families, they wish they could take a long holiday, they wish they could own a boat or a huge house or fly around the world first class. But nothing will materialize simply because you wish for it. **Stop wishing for things and commit to achieving them.**

Vince: *I meet so many people who have a sort-of-want attitude. It's all "I sort of want to be wealthy," or "I think I'd like to achieve financial freedom." Absolutely nothing is going to happen for you when you are in this mode. Until you* ***make a commitment*** *to what you want, until you decide "this is what I want," you will wander around in circles achieving nothing. People walk into our seminars looking half-dead. They walk out at the end with their eyes alight with passion, totally committed to doing what it takes to get what they want. I love seeing the change in people when they suddenly get that fire in their bellies and make that commitment to achieving their greatest desires.*

2. Ready, Fire, Aim

In other words, never procrastinate. Do it *now.* Most people spend their lives saying, "Ready, aim . . . ready, aim . . . ready, aim . . . " They get nowhere. It would be better to fire and miss than never to fire at all. We certainly don't mean to suggest that you should skip the *ready* step; that must be your first concern. You have to get all your ducks in a row and arm yourself with all your preparation; but once you *are* ready, don't sit around waiting for the perfect target or perfect time, because it may not come or you may not recognize it. Every time you fire, even if you miss, you get experience. The more experience you get, the closer you will come to hitting the bull's-eye one day.

Vince: *"Ready, fire, aim" is one of John's favourite sayings, and at face value it looks like it contradicts our advice to get educated, but the education bit is included in the "ready." We're not saying, "Fire, ready, aim" we're saying get* ready *(i.e., get all the education you need and prepare yourself) and then take action. If you don't hit the target, look again at your preparation, make a couple of adjustments, and fire again. You can't always wait for the target to present itself because you might not know where it is until you fire a few times! It's really about not procrastinating simply because you're not 100 percent sure what the outcome of your actions will be. Obviously, you* must *have all your preparation (your education, your financing, etc.) in place before you fire.*

John: *For years I'd been saying I wanted to learn to play the guitar but I kept putting it off, making excuses like I didn't have time, that I hadn't found a teacher, or that I probably wouldn't be any good at it. Finally, about six months ago, I just went out and bought a guitar and gave it a go every day. Every day I tried to pluck and strum the strings. No one taught me; I taught myself. For months it sounded terrible. My fingers were red and raw* *and even bled sometimes; it was incredibly painful. But I kept going and my fingertips got tougher. Now I can play some pretty decent chords; I can pluck and strum the guitar. It's given me an amazing sense of accomplishment.*

Until you pull that trigger, nothing is going to happen. So forget about aiming, just take a crapshoot. Pull the trigger and see what you hit. If you get it wrong, try again and keep firing until you hit your target. Failing is just finding another path that doesn't lead to your destination. The more times you fail, the closer you are to finding the right path. However, don't be stubborn. Don't ignore your failures; you must still learn and accept the ways you *can't* achieve your dreams. Going down the same path when you know it dead ends is not smart. As Albert Einstein said, the definition of insanity is doing the same thing over and over again and expecting different results.

Yes, timing has a lot to do with success, but you must take action and keep taking action, and when your action doesn't produce the results you need, you must take a slightly different action.

We like to modify the title of Napoleon Hill's seminal book, *Think and Grow Rich*; we say, ***Do** and Grow Rich.*

John: *You've got to get in the game and keep shooting at goal. Some people like to sit at the game and spectate. That's a nice relaxing position to be in. But as a spectator, you're only ever going to be celebrating someone else's goals. Other people get into the game but they don't know which side they're on. They keep playing defensively to hedge their bets. But if you play defensively all the time, you can never win. Other people kick the ball around but they have no idea where the goalposts are. If you want to achieve things in life, get onto the pitch, figure out where the goalposts are, get the ball and kick it at goal. It doesn't matter if you miss as long as you try. Even Luis Suarez, the top goal scorer in the English Premier League during the 2013–2014 season, misses plenty of times. Keep going back and getting the ball, and keep kicking until you start scoring goals. Then guess what? The confidence and excitement you get from scoring your first few goals will help you go on and score more. But you must still make sure you are fit and warmed up before getting on the pitch in the first place!*

3. Do Whatever It Takes

Obviously we are not advocating criminal or morally corrupt behaviour, but within the bounds of what is morally decent and legal, you have to be prepared to do things that feel uncomfortable. Do we like making endless phone calls and negotiating deals? Not really. Do we enjoy dealing with the problems of tenants, or chasing rent arrears? No. But these unpleasant things have to be done when you are running a property business. Life is not designed to be a bed of roses. And even roses have thorns. If you want to enjoy these beautiful flowers, you have to risk getting scratched. Not everyone is prepared to go through that pain; not everyone will go that extra distance. If you ask Olympic athletes, they will tell you that what usually separates them from the ones who don't qualify is just the sheer number of training hours they put in. You may have to do very unglamorous things in order to have a glamorous lifestyle. But, as we keep saying, before you get the things you want, you have to go through the discomfort.

Vince: *Doing property deals is hardly a glamorous way to spend your time. It can be tedious and extremely frustrating. Tenants can be a nightmare. You can have a property standing empty for months while you try to find a tenant for it, and all the while you have to keep paying the mortgage on it. You have to do things well outside of your comfort zone. You hear no a lot. You have to chase people who disappear, deal with incompetent people who let you down, get angry with lawyers who drag their feet. I can put weeks of work into negotiating a deal, and suddenly the seller will go AWOL and no one can find him and it's all been for nothing. This is* not *easy street. But these are the things you have to do. You go through the pain, you learn the hard way, and then you get better at it, because you know it will all bring you closer to your goals.*

4. Never, Never, Never Give Up

"Never, never, never give up" are the famous words of Sir Winston Churchill, whose attitude saved Britain from falling into the hands of a German dictator. You have to be prepared to die trying to achieve what you want. If you give up before you die, you are cheating yourself. What would be the point of living then? Life is about completing a series of achievements; to live otherwise means you are not *living*, you are simply *existing*. There should be no quitting until the final curtain. While you live and breathe, you have another chance. Whatever life has dealt you, you still have another chance. Never, never, never give up.

Vince: *Nothing speaks to me more on this point than the story about the man who gave up when he was three feet from finding gold. The story goes that a man from the East Coast wanted to get in on the California gold rush. He invested all his money in the necessary equipment, transported it all west, hired people to work for him and started digging. He kept digging for two years. He used up all his money, all his friends' money, got into debt and eventually gave up. He sold all his equipment to another guy and threw in the towel. The first day the second guy started digging he struck gold after going three feet. The first guy invested all that time and money, and gave up when he was three feet from hitting gold. Never, never, never,* never *give up!*

John: *A more recent story that always inspires me is Sylvester Stallone's story of getting* Rocky *made. It's fairly well known that before Stallone sold the rights to* Rocky *he was completely broke. He was so hard up he actually sold his dog for $50. Finally he was offered serious money for the film rights to his screenplay on the condition that he step away from playing the starring role. He said no. It's said that the producers offered him well over a quarter of a million dollars for the rights as long as he gave up the right to star in it. Stallone kept saying no. He knew the film was his best chance of becoming a star. Eventually the producers gave in, offering him a fraction of the money for the rights, but allowing him to star in it. The rest, as they say, is history!*

5. Learn from the Best and Pay for the Best

Every successful entrepreneur from Alan Sugar to Richard Branson will probably tell you the same thing. If you want to be successful, find someone who's got to where you want to be and copy his or her methods until you work out your own. You won't take exactly the same path as your mentor, because you will encounter your own issues and deal with your own personal shortcomings, but you may save yourself some valuable time, and avoid a few pitfalls, by listening to and learning from someone who has been through their own ups and downs on the path to success. Everyone's journey in life is unique. Evolution is progression. It's all about taking what's gone before and making it better. We hope your path is easier than our paths were; we hope you're *more* successful than we are. That's the point of life, to keep improving, to keep growing and doing things better. And when you find the best teacher, you must be prepared to pay for your education; don't ask for it for free.

John: *There's this story about a FedEx conveyer belt breaking down. The company was losing business by the second with the holdups. Someone heard about an expert engineer who specialized in fixing conveyer belts and managed to get hold of him. The guy shows up and examines the belt for a while, then takes out a screw, replaces it, and turns the belt on again. It works perfectly. The guys at FedEx were very grateful until the engineer gave them his bill for $10,000. They said, "Wait, there must be a mistake; this bill says $10,000 and all you did was change a screw." The engineer smiled and said, "Yes, it was $1 for the screw and $9,999 for knowing which screw to change."*

6. Have the Highest Standards

We love that old saying, "**How you do anything is how you do everything.**" If you live in chaos, your business is bound to be in chaos. If you have a habit of cutting corners in one area of your life, you could easily unconsciously cut corners in another. In *A New Earth*, Ekhart Tolle talks about doing the washing up for the sake of doing the washing up, and doing it well. Even if you usually throw everything in the dishwasher to save time, it's not a bad idea sometimes to take the time to wash the dishes, to iron a shirt instead of paying someone to do it for you, to prepare a healthy meal with care instead of defrosting a ready meal in four minutes or picking up the phone to order a takeaway. By occasionally doing menial tasks and doing them well, we are training ourselves to pay attention to detail, a vital skill for building a successful business. When Steve Jobs caught an engineer putting together a circuit board messily, he asked the engineer to do it again and make it as neat as possible. The guy asked why, since no one was going to see it. Jobs replied, with words to the effect of, "I'm going to see it, and you're going to see it." He viewed the circuit board as a work of art and therefore felt it should look the best it could possibly look. He used to get people who had worked on a particular project to sign a piece of paper that was then stuck onto the circuit board. Even though the circuit board was to be sealed up and no one would see it, Jobs felt that the fact that the engineers had to put their names on it would make them work to their highest standards.

7. Make Sacrifices

If you can't make sacrifices to build a financially abundant future, then we don't believe you deserve one. We're always astonished by the kind of excuses we hear. People give the lamest excuses as to why they can't get to a seminar, let alone why they can't invest in a new business venture. What they are really saying is that they're not prepared to make the time to start improving their lives. People act as if they are being *pushed* into learning about building their wealth. If you don't want to build your wealth, and if you're not prepared to make the necessary sacrifices, then don't do it! If you want it, make sacrifices. It's that simple!

8. Take Risks

By risk, we do not mean a gamble. Taking all your money and putting it on black in roulette is not taking a risk; it's gambling. Taking a risk is doing the right research on a property, deciding that there is a good chance that you will make a profit, and investing in it, even though you know there is a chance you might fail. You've weighed up the odds and you've decided that the chance of winning outweighs the chance of losing. (And even losing doesn't mean losing everything.) People think about investing in property and they see all the risks involved. But do you know what is a bigger risk? *Not* taking that risk. Doing nothing is the biggest risk you could take. Leaving your future in the hands of your employer and simply trusting that you will never be made redundant, assuming your pension plan will be enough to support you when you retire, believing someone will help you out if you get sick and are incapacitated and unable to work... these are much bigger risks than risking acquiring assets to bring in a passive income.

9. Do What Others Won't to Have a Tomorrow Others Don't

"Do what others won't to have a tomorrow others don't" is one of our favourite sayings because it sums up what we are about. It sums up everything we are talking about here. It's not an easy ride: Most people won't put in the hours and the effort, or muster the courage to do what it takes. But if you do, your future will be very different from what you see your contemporaries experiencing. Laziness in Britain seems to be contagious, but you must protect yourself. It's not okay to sit around and expect to be given a living without working for it when you are perfectly able bodied and capable. Our welfare system, once the pride of our nation, has been seriously abused. We are now seen as a soft touch around the world; a place where anyone can turn up and be given food and shelter without having to work. There's a dangerous sense of entitlement spreading through the country. The only thing we believe everyone is *entitled* to is the opportunity to work hard and earn a living. But working hard *is* hard work. Remember, there's no baby without the pain!

10. Give Back

Earlier we said that you can't skip any steps to becoming financially abundant. While this is technically true, you *can* adopt the mindset of a financially abundant person. It's good practice and it trains your mind to think differently about money. Even if it's a small amount that you are giving away—perhaps by giving a generous tip, making a donation to a charitable cause, or making an impulsive gesture to help someone out, it symbolizes your expectation that you can *afford* to do it. Be sensible, of course. Make sure your financial commitments are covered before you give money away, but *do* give money away when you can. The amount you give will then increase according to your budget. And this concept doesn't just apply to money. Give a little time when you can afford to do so, too. Give some time to someone in need, to someone who can benefit from your knowledge and compassion. Again, the more you build your passive income, the more you buy back your time, and the more time (in time!) you will have to give.

People are so reluctant to let go of their possessions; they cling onto what they have as if they could hold onto it forever. But nothing lasts forever. One day we're all going to be dead, and our possessions will either have been destroyed through wear and tear or will belong to someone else. We're only borrowing everything we have for our short lifetimes. Most people live in a very parochial way, with set limits, believing that they cannot and should not expect more.

There is always more . . . if you want it.

Additional Top Tips for Success

Finally, here are a few more of our favourite sayings.

Your *network* is your *net worth.*

No great business was built without great partnerships. The people you do business with, the people you include in your business, the people you hire and the people you serve are all part of your network. Take care of it; it is a major part of what you are worth. Treat your staff and customers with great respect. Respect and value your business partnerships, and do not put up with people who do not respect you. The money is in the relationships; the fortune is in the follow-ups.

Think *big*.

You have to start thinking *big* instead of small. (Donald Trump says if you're going to do some thinking about investing anyway, you might as well make it *big*!) Imagine the size of the return on your investment. How big do you want it to be? If you want it to be sizeable, then you have to put in the proportional amount of work, in terms of money and time. Your investment is your money and your time. You have to give as much as you can to your project before you get anything back. Of course that's scary, but you won't get your return if you don't do it. Three things that can help you are:

Motivational tools. We still have our occasional down days when we struggle to keep the faith. We have various short films and audio clips we look at and listen to during these times that get us back on track and keep us focused. At the time of writing, our favourite is a YouTube video that has received over 25 million hits to date. It features a voice-over of a speech by the Hip Hop Preacher, Eric Thomas, and incredible footage of the American football star Giavanni Ruffin in training. Do a search for it and watch it. It's called "How Bad Do You Want It? (Success)."

Your wealth plan. You must have a plan written down; you must know what your daily tasks are. Your plan is your own personal charter. You set your goals and then you write down all the steps you plan to take in order to achieve your goals; you write down every single thing you need to do on your way to achieving your goals. You need to specify, in writing, exactly what you have to do and when you have to do it. Every day you should have a list of things you have to do from your plan. If you wake up in the morning and you don't know what you're supposed to be doing towards achieving your goals, you are not going to get very far.

Accountability. If you are struggling to stick to your plan, write a list of the things you know you should be doing and next to each one write down the reason you are not doing that thing. Be honest with yourself. You are probably living in Excuseville. Your problem is that you have no one to answer to but yourself. So *give* yourself someone to answer to. Just ask a friend to hold you accountable. Facebook is a great place for holding yourself accountable. We know someone who quit smoking and was greatly helped by posting every day on Facebook the number of days he'd been smoke-free. In doing this he got encouragement from all his friends who began posting their congratulations. Another friend was training for a marathon and said she may have given up were it not for the fact that she posted every training milestone (each new record distance) on her Facebook page; she practically lived for the huge encouragement she got from friends and family. Make yourself accountable and you will see a huge difference in what you achieve.

All the knowledge you need is right at your fingertips.

There are seminal books that you must read if you want to change your life for the better. Books such as *Feel the Fear and Do It Anyway* by Susan Jeffers, *The 7 Habits of Highly Effective People* by Stephen R. Covey, and, more recently, Walter Isaacson's biography of Steve Jobs, include many of the keys to successful thinking. It's all about mindset. But you must practice what these books preach. You could easily read your way to success...as long as you implement what you learn. Don't buy these books and let them sit on your shelf; don't let them become what we call *shelf*-development books. Never stop reading and learning. There is no end to learning; there is always more to learn. And however much you learn, you will still make mistakes, but you may as well save time by not making the same mistakes that others have made! If you're not reading *Forbes*, you should be reading *Forbes*. If you are going to be financially successful, you have to read what financially successful people are reading and read about what they are doing.

Action creates *attraction.*

Like the ripples that occur in a pond when you throw a stone into it and break the clear surface, every action you take has a butterfly effect. The little waves we make when we take action create ripples in the universe and we attract back to us the results of those actions. Watch the ripples on the pond after you've thrown in a stone. At first it seems as if they are only moving outwards, but if you look carefully you'll see miniature circular waves being cast back to the centre. For every action there is a reaction. So the message here is . . . **keep taking action**!

> Experience is the child of thought, and thought is the child of action.
>
> —Benjamin Disraeli

Conclusion: The Now

I've failed over and over and over again in my life, and that is why I succeed.

—Michael Jordan

If you talk to any successful person, he or she will tell you that the journey is far more exciting than the destination. In fact, there is no destination. If you set a goal and achieve it, your next job is to set a new goal. Life is not about reaching a place and standing still in it for the rest of time. That is often the big mistake made by lottery winners and people who inherit a fortune. They believe that the money is the answer, they stop setting goals, they stop striving to achieve something out of their comfort zone ... they stagnate. It's not about the destination; it's always about the journey ... so keep setting off on new ones.

Are we still taking journeys and challenging ourselves today? Absolutely. Do we still make mistakes and fail? Every day. We climb a mountain, reach the summit and then look for a new mountain to conquer. Life is full of possibilities; you can't even exhaust a fraction of them in one lifetime, so experience as much as you can.

Vince: *From a very young age, I had a conviction that I was destined to achieve big things. I saw myself as being incredibly wealthy and successful. I couldn't clearly imagine exactly what I'd be successful at—and maybe that's why I've had an eclectic career, going from child actor, to pharmacist, to property investor and business owner—but I never lost the faith that I was going to be very successful at* something. *And perhaps that is what has kept me going, kept me getting up again each time I get knocked down. Any successful person will tell you that the journey of life doesn't go in a straight line. That was definitely my experience. For many years it was just blood, sweat, and tears, and there were many times when I thought I'd lost sight of the light at the end of the tunnel. But I never let life beat me. I took the punches and kept* *moving forward, and today I'm exactly where I'd set my sights. I am financially free, I have a number of thriving businesses, and I have a beautiful wife and amazing children.*

There was one turning point I will never forget. I think the fact that the incident had a direct impact on the people closest to me motivated me more than anything else in my life had ever done.

About eight years ago now, when Annika and I had been married only a short time and our daughter, Hannah, was still just a baby, things were still quite bleak financially speaking. I hadn't recovered from the collapse of my first business and I was struggling to build my next one. We had just moved up to Milton Keynes and I was pretty depressed. London had been my home since arriving in England when I was a child and I was finding it hard to adjust. I knew Milton Keynes was going to be a better place to raise a family, but I missed London and my friends.

I was working at my computer, at home, when Annika and Hannah came through the door. I knew immediately that something was wrong. Annika had gone out shopping but she'd returned without any bags. I asked her where the shopping was and she burst into tears. She'd gone round the supermarket, filled a shopping trolley with food, gone to the checkout, bagged it all up, and then tried to pay. Her debit card was refused. She tried a credit card; that was refused. She tried another card and that one was also declined. She had to leave her shopping behind and walk out of the shop in shame. I was horrified. I promised her that it would never happen again. I started working harder than I'd ever worked in my life. I made a solemn vow to ensure that my family would always be comfortable and secure. I have never looked back. Today I have fulfilled that promise, and I intend to ensure that I continue to do so.

Very early in our relationship Annika had said to me, "It doesn't matter what we have, I love you. If we end up living in a council house, I'll still love you. As long as we have each other, I'm happy." Maybe that had let me off the hook for a while. Perhaps I'd used that as an excuse to say to myself that it wouldn't matter if we ended up without a solid financial foundation. All I know is that when I saw my wife suffer the embarrassment and shock of not being able to pay for groceries, it was like someone lit a fire in my pants. I was not going to rest until I could guarantee that it would never, ever *happen again!*

During one of my darkest moments I remembered a speech from the film Rocky Balboa, *in which Rocky is talking to his son. He says,*

> Let me tell you something you already know. The world ain't all sunshine and rainbows. It's a very mean and nasty place, and I

> don't care how tough you are, it will beat you to your knees and keep you there permanently if you let it. You, me, or nobody is gonna hit as hard as life. But it ain't about how hard you hit. It's about how hard you can get hit and keep moving forward; how much you can take and keep moving forward. That's how winning is done! Now, if you know what you're worth, then go out and get what you're worth. But you gotta be willing to take the hits, and not be pointing fingers saying you ain't where you wanna be because of him, or her, or anybody. Cowards do that and that ain't you. You're better than that!

I learnt that speech by heart and repeated it to myself whenever things got tough. I worked through the bad days and slowly but surely came to realize that when you fail massively, you also gain massively. What you lose in terms of money and pride, you gain in experience and transferable skills. Even if your skills don't fit the model you applied them to initially, you can take them with you into the next venture and they might be exactly the skills that turn out to bring you huge success. You can lose money, but you can't lose skills. This challenged everything I'd been taught by my Chinese heritage. Suddenly I knew that losing face through losing money was actually important, because it was humbling. It was not something to fear; it was inevitable. Once I fully accepted this belief and applied it to my work every day, I never looked back.

The funny thing is, once I had ensured that my family was safe and secure, I wanted to help other people. I knew the relief I'd felt having provided for my family and I wanted others to experience that feeling. I love speaking at seminars and I love teaching people how to improve their businesses and how to make the most profit from property investing, but nothing fulfils me more than helping people turn their lives around. When someone approaches me to tell me that something I *have done—whether it was selling them a couple of leads or inspiring them at a seminar—has fundamentally changed their lives, it means everything to me.*

A young man stood up recently, at one of our Wealth Dragon introductory seminars and said, "I've always been broke, my mum and dad have always been broke, so I thought there was something wrong with me; I thought there was something wrong with them. But now I know they just didn't have any education about wealth. How could they have taught me anything about managing my money and getting financially free when they didn't know anything themselves? Now I know there's nothing wrong with them and there's nothing wrong with me; I just need to get a bit of financial education and put it into practice. When I've done that, I know I'm going to transform my life and *the lives of my parents."*

That's what I'm in it for now, to hear stories like that.

At this point in time I have everything I want. I have a great business partner, thriving businesses, a nice house to live in, and enough money to provide for my family and enjoy holidays with them. I get quality time with my kids, I pack lunch boxes and do the school run; I'm a big part of their lives. If I were working 12 hours a day for a big investment bank in the city, I couldn't do these things. I still miss London but I've come to enjoy living in the countryside a little way outside Milton Keynes. It's a good environment for my children—Hannah and my son, Lewis, who was born in 2008. We have good schools, a good transport system, nice shops, and a close community feeling. And there are cows (real cows!) grazing in the field behind my home.

There are plenty of people in my life who have a different outlook from me. Their perspective is more along the lines of: we all end up in the same place (the grave), so why worry about acquiring much wealth while we're alive. Well, I may end up in a dusty grave, but I don't want to live there now*! I don't need to be immortalized or remembered long after my death. It doesn't matter to me one way or another because I won't be around to see it. What matters to me is that I make the absolute best of my life while I have it. I believe the universe is always expanding, and I just want to expand and grow with it. I want to make a difference now, while I'm alive to see that difference take shape. That's what gets me up in the mornings: the opportunity to learn and grow; that's the heartbeat of my life. The only legacy I care about leaving is that when I'm gone, my wife and children remember me as a good husband and father, respectively.*

John: *Family means everything to me, and Vincent Wong is family to me; he's like a brother. We've been through more together than I've been through with any other person. We nearly died in a car accident together once. Experiences like that bond you for life. We've been through it all together—in business and in our personal lives. In fact, if it wasn't for something Vince said to me when I was in the midst of a personal crisis, I wouldn't be the person I am today.*

Three years ago I was about to get married. The venue had been booked, the invitations had been sent out, the relatives had booked their flights from China; everything was set for a very lavish weekend. It should have been the happiest time of my life, but I was miserable. All my fiancée and I did was argue. We couldn't agree on anything. I thought I loved her and I believed she loved me, but our daily lives were full of negativity and niggling irritations.

It was about two weeks before the wedding and Vince took me to the pub after work for a drink. He asked me if I was feeling okay and I said, "No. Not really." He was used to a lot of positivity from me, so this shocked him.

Vince: *I remember this day like it was yesterday. John had been looking ill for weeks. He was pale and had dark circles under his eyes. His face was set in a permanent frown. I knew he wasn't happy in his relationship but I couldn't just say, "Dude, don't marry her." So I told him about my first wedding and how down I had been feeling at the time. My first wife and I had been arguing constantly in the run up to the wedding. I was growing more and more depressed, but I couldn't back out: I knew a lot of money had been spent on the wedding. In the end I decided I had to go through with it, figuring I could always get divorced down the line. I remember standing outside the church in a little Welsh village with my dad. He could see I wasn't happy. He said to me, "Son, we can leave right now if you want, you don't need to go through with it." I nearly took him up on the offer; I probably would have done except that I suddenly remembered that I was partly marrying this Welsh woman to piss him off him in the first place! So I went through with the wedding and things just went from bad to worse. Even though I ended up getting the divorce I'd predicted a year later, it was a year of sheer hell. If you're imagining your divorce on your wedding day, it's probably not a good sign!*

John: *After Vince told me his story in the pub I went straight round to my mum and dad's place and told them I wasn't going through with the wedding. I said I wasn't in love with my fiancée anymore and didn't believe we'd be happy together. Unlike Vince's dad, my father tried to force me into it by issuing an ultimatum. He was furious. He said, "Either you get married or you are no longer my son." As Vince explained earlier, Chinese culture is all about saving face. My own father threatened to disown me rather than lose face because his son had run out on his fiancée. But Vince had shown me that you can't live your life in retrospect or regret. I broke off the engagement. It was the hardest decision I have ever made. I cried my eyes out. I'd never been so miserable. I was a millionaire, but I felt more worthless than I'd ever felt when I'd been broke. I was empty.*

After that I went AWOL. I actually ran away to Malaysia. I stayed in Kuala Lumpur for several months pissing away as much money as I could. No one knew where I was. I did nothing but gamble. I used to go into casinos with the aim of losing money. It was just something to do. I didn't know what to live for; I was so depressed. That was when I realized that money definitely didn't guarantee you happiness. But thankfully I did finally come to my senses and returned home.

I just walked back into the Wealth Dragons office one day. Everyone fell silent and stared at me. They hadn't known whether I was alive or dead. After what felt like a minute, but was probably only about 20 seconds, they all burst into applause. That night we all went out for dinner. I remember Florence, Vince's sister, toasting me and telling me I'd just grown a new pair of balls!

When he inadvertently stopped me from making the biggest mistake of my life, Vince gave me a new lease on life (once I'd gone through my self-destruct phase!). I got back on track, worked on myself, and eventually met my current partner, Jennifer, with whom I have the most wonderful, calm, positive relationship. We were married in September 2014. This time it was a wedding I looked forward to and relished every moment of. I am right where I want to be. And it was worth every ounce of pain it took to get here.

Life needs a design. If you're not designing your life, someone else is doing it for you.

We can so easily live our lives all boxed up. We sleep in box-shaped beds, in box-shaped rooms. We watch box-shaped TVs and drive to work in box-shaped cars before sitting in our box-shaped offices in front of our box-shaped computers while we talk on our box-shaped phones. That isn't living, it's just existing. I was all set for a boxed-in life before Vince shook me up and gave me permission to break out and run for the hills.

I am indebted to Vince. Whenever I hang out with Vince and his family, I look at his children and think how amazing they are. Lewis is only six years old, but he's already very articulate and knowledgeable. Hannah is now ten years old and is already a little businesswoman. Sometimes I think they already understand more about life than we do. And isn't that the point? Each generation must *improve on the one that has gone before; life must be lived forwards. Our legacy is to pass on what we know to the children, so that they can develop that knowledge even further. If you don't take everything you know and pass it on to someone to share with the world, you are doing future generations a disservice. Information is the most powerful commodity we have. Change doesn't happen when you build a new house or make another million, it happens when you alter the way the world thinks. Take everything you know and give it to children, and then encourage them to go out and learn more. None of this is about us; it is all about the next generation; it's about what we can learn now that we can pass on, in order to help the next generation to grow beyond where we left off.*

Education is the key to success.

Vince: *That, and building a business with your best friend.*

> If we listened to our intellect, we'd never have a love affair. We'd never have a friendship. We'd never go into business, because we'd be cynical. Well, that's nonsense. You've got to jump off cliffs all the time and build your wings on the way down.
>
> —Ray Bradbury

Final Word

At the beginning of this book, we asked why you had picked it up and suggested it might be because you wanted to be free of money worries. We hope we've succeeded in not only helping you expand your *why*, but also in showing you *how* it is possible. We also asked *when* you wanted to start to live like this. We hope the answer is . . .

Now!

*   *   *

To contact us, please visit our website
www.wealthdragons.co.uk.

You can e-mail us at
info@wealthdragons.co.uk
or call
+44 (0)1908 69 88 60.

Index